— EVEN MORE —
GHOST STORIES
of
ALBERTA

Barbara Smith

Lone Pine Publishing

The Publisher: Lone Pine Publishing
10145 – 81 Avenue
Edmonton, AB T6E 1W9
Canada

Website: http://www.lonepinepublishing.com

National Library of Canada Cataloguing in Publication Data

Smith, Barbara, 1947–
    Even more Alberta ghost stories

    ISBN 1-55105-323-3

    1. Ghosts—Alberta. 2. Legends—Alberta. I. Title.
GR580.S6216 2001   398.2'09712305   C2001-910760-9

Editorial Director: Nancy Foulds
Project Editor: Shelagh Kubish
Production Manager: Jody Reekie
Book Design: Arlana Anderson-Hale
Cover Design: Robert Weidemann
Layout & Production: Arlana Anderson-Hale

Photo Credits: The photographs in this book are reproduced with the generous permis-
sion of their owners. W. Ritchie Benedict (p. 225, p. 226); Glenbow Archives, Calgary,
Canada, #NA-2365-23 (p. 153); #ND-8-282 (p. 157); #NA-5464-1 (p. 185); Barry Hunter
(p. 11); Kuerbis family (p. 101); Nordstrom family (p. 123); Barbara Smith (p. 50, p. 116);
Robert Smith (p. 9, p. 66, p. 134); Treasure Chest and Antiques Limited (p. 191); Deborah
Trumbley (p. 204). Other photos have been contributed on the condition of anonymity.

The stories, folklore and legends in this book are based on the author's collection of
sources including individuals whose experiences have led them to believe they have
encountered phenomena of some kind or another. They are meant to entertain, and
neither the publisher nor the author claims these stories represent fact.

We acknowledge the financial support of the Government of Canada through the Book
Publishing Industry Development Program (BPIDP) for our publishing activities.

PC: P6

Dedication

This book is dedicated, with thanks,

to the people of this province.

Contents

Chapter Five: Spirit's Inn

Chapter Six: Alberta Anomalies

Acknowledgements

I would like to begin by acknowledging the tremendous contribution so many Albertans have made to my projects. To all of you who have read my books or who have taken the time to write to me, either with a comment or to share an experience, thank you. To those who have stopped to exchange a friendly word at a book signing or at a presentation of some kind, thank you. Your support, generosity and thoughtfulness have been deeply appreciated.

Thank you, too, to those who have contributed directly to this volume—those whose names are mentioned in their individual stories and those who have chosen to remain anonymous.

In addition I wish to thank Elizabeth J. Allan, Carole Bambullis, Steve Bartlett, W. Ritchie Benedict, Kim Buehler, Ron Hlady, Leslie Holth, Jan Jones, Barbara Leonard, Betty Knight, Hilary Munro, Teresa Phillips, Rob Reid, Tracy Roberts, Christina Tower, Lisa Schlegel, Collin Schofield, Laura Seymour, Michelle Simick, G. Smith, Kathy Smith, Katharina Thomas, the staff at CBC Radio and the staff at the Glenbow Archives.

Thanks, always, to those closest to me—my husband, Bob Smith, my daughters, Debbie and Robyn, my fellow authors and dear friends Jo-Anne Christensen and Dr. Barrie Robinson. Your love and support keep me going and make everything worthwhile. And finally, thank you to everyone at Lone Pine Publishing. It is an honour to work with such a skilled group of people. My sincere thanks to you all, especially Shane Kennedy, Nancy Foulds, Shelagh Kubish and Arlana Anderson-Hale.

Introduction

Although this is my 11th book of true ghost stories, I'm still not able to answer many of the questions I set out with a decade ago. For instance, are ghosts external or internal to those who encounter them? It would seem there is not one arbitrarily correct answer to that question. Hauntings are unique, and as such, are probably each caused by a unique set of circumstances.

When a person sees an apparition, for instance, has that manifestation popped into the witness's reality, or has the observer stepped into the ghost's time and place? Again, I don't believe that a blanket explanation can be adequate.

To my mind, however, this lack of consistency does not make the experience, or the ghost, any less real. I once received a very nice letter from someone who was certain that "Oscar," the resident spirit who tormented workers at the radio station in Canadian Forces Base, Cold Lake, was created as a practical joke. First of all, in this case especially, I do wonder if that is correct, as I have some pretty impressive documentation about that haunting. But, second, and perhaps more important, I think the key word in the interpretation is "created." An entity was "created." If anyone doubts that possibility, I refer them to the story "Philip, the Carefully Constructed Phantom" in my book *Ontario Ghost Stories.*

I have also spoken to a retired school teacher who told me that he "created" (there's that word again!) "Peter," the predominant ghost in Edmonton's McKay Avenue School

Peter is still marked "present" at this school.

(Edmonton Public Schools Museum and Archives) in order to illustrate a philosophy that he wanted his students to understand. Well, if this is so, that man was certainly successful in at least one regard, for Peter, along with a collection of other spirits, is still very much a presence in the old red brick school building, as I discussed in my 1993 book *Ghost Stories of Alberta*. Despite such certainty in that regard, one error in the story does need to be corrected. The 1881 School House that shares the schoolyard with the "newer" building was *not* used as a tool shed during Peter's life. The small clapboard building had been moved and was being used as a house during that period, so what forces Ron Hlady, Building Preservation Technician at McKay, occasionally reacts to when he goes into the older building remain a mystery.

There are many other fascinating possibilities to ponder. For instance, geological engineer Steve Bartlett suggests that events in our lives leave imprints upon aural energy fields. Perhaps ghosts are merely activations of those aural archives. Dramatic events (especially death) will "crystal-lize" psychic (or aural) energy so that, "instead of flowing, like a hot liquid, [the energy] will undergo a forced change," freeze or set in place, causing manifestations beyond that which we can normally sense. Or, in a word, ghosts. He might be right. The theory is certainly thought provoking. If you are interested in more discussion and definitions related to the paranormal, you could read the introduction to my book *More Ghost Stories of Alberta* (1996).

As a matter of fact, I find all of this most interesting to ponder, but I am not a paranormal expert by any means. I am a storyteller with a special affection for the combination of history and mystery, hence my inherent delight in researching and writing local ghost lore for my readers to enjoy. Whether or not we *ever* answer any deep and meaningful questions is, I think, secondary to that. So, sit back, relax and please do enjoy this new collection of Alberta ghost stories.

Chapter 1

Haunted Houses

*Home is where we go to feel safe and protected from the world. Unfortunately, home cannot always protect us from the forces of the **other** world.*

Horrifying Haunting

The supernatural events described in this retelling took place in central Alberta in a friendly rural community where most people know one another. Although the haunted house has now been abandoned, it still stands. The owners, however, have vowed that they will never again let anyone tour the old place on their property.

"We've lived all our lives in this area. We've had people coming from the schools, and from the cities, wanting to look at the house or walk through it. At first we were saying that it was okay but we're not letting anybody in anymore," my contact explained. In order to respect their decision and privacy, we agreed that the couple be referred to as John and Linda and that the exact location of their home not be pinpointed.

John began by explaining, "We don't know for sure when the place was built. We know it was in existence in 1907, as a dance hall and a way station for wagons travelling to town for supplies. My parents bought [the property] in 1946."

John and his brother grew up in the place, but didn't know it was haunted.

"When we were kids obviously our parents didn't want to scare us. My mother just mentioned a few things. She never did like the house. We have a sun porch on one corner of the house and she said, 'I don't like this room' and always kept the door closed. She put the piano in front of it so we couldn't go in there. She didn't like the basement either," John recalled.

Maybe the family would have eventually discussed their unusual surroundings but, unfortunately, John's parents

The family that used to live here is afraid to tear the house down, in case any of the entities that once haunted it come looking for another home—theirs.

died when he was a teenager. "We didn't get a chance to talk about it," the man acknowledged.

Despite this missed opportunity, John does know the history of the area and of what is now his property. Before his parents bought it, "there was some trouble in the house. It [went] up for sale quite quickly. The owners just kind of left first and then sold it."

The motivation behind John and Linda's insistence on anonymity became understandable as they related their experiences in the old house. Linda moved into the homestead as a newlywed in 1966. She explained, "Things started when we got married, fairly soon after I moved in. I got locked out one day; I went out to the clothesline and the door closed and locked behind me."

With that symbolic unwelcoming gesture from the spirits in her new home, the bride's adventures in the haunted house began. John added, "From the day we were married, Linda always felt like she was intruding in the house. She just chalked it up to moving into a fully furnished home."

Unfortunately, as their experiences were to bear out, the explanation was not that simple. On a day when John was away, Linda heard a persistent knocking sound coming from the basement. After hours of listening to the unremitting noise, Linda pushed the racket from her conscious mind. "Of course, when John came home he asked what the noise was. I told him that I didn't know but that it had been happening all day."

The man went down to the basement to investigate but, aside from determining which of the walls the sound seemed to be coming from, he came back upstairs still puzzled. The couple endured that particular anomaly often enough that they were able to describe it in detail and yet never able to determine its source. John explained, "The knocking sounded like it was coming from the basement, from the cement wall on the north side. You could hear it through most of the house. It was about the speed of someone hammering a nail."

Whatever spectral energy they were sharing the house with had many more complex tricks left to perform. Furniture in the house, for instance, began moving on its own. "The first thing was an old-style tri-light lamp that slid partway across the floor, fell over and smashed."

Initially, the couple suspected that their cat had knocked over the light, but Linda confirmed "the cat was outside."

The cat may not have been responsible for the lamp moving and falling, but the animal was certainly aware of the ghostly inhabitants. One day, as Linda and John watched, "the cat was asleep on the couch. He woke up suddenly and just started watching from the door in the corner of the living room. The cat watched something move across the room. He was standing straight up with his tail straight up and with his hair straight out. I was wondering what the cat was watching," John recalled. "I couldn't see anything."

Although John and Linda accepted that they lived in a haunted house, the ghosts were still capable of startling the pair. John related one particularly chilling incident.

"We had company in for cards one evening. It was nine thirty or ten o'clock. We were all sitting at the table playing cards and chatting when these footsteps started, heavy footsteps from upstairs. They were loud enough that all four of us stopped and listened to them. The other fellow and myself, we grabbed shotguns and went upstairs because we were sure there was somebody up there. There was nobody up there though," he explained before adding this additional goosebump factor: "The room these footsteps were going across upstairs was a [crowded] storage room. There's no possible way that *anyone* could've walked across that room. The hair on the back of my neck was standing straight up. The fellow who was with me never did go into that room. He was just shaking on the stairs."

Unlike many people who live with ghosts, neither John nor Linda had any definite sense of their ghosts' genders, although the heaviness of the footsteps they heard led them to believe that at least one of the phantoms was a man.

From this point the paranormal activity became stranger and stranger. Linda described how they once listened to the sound of "things falling down the stairs—the very obvious sound of something heavy tumbling down the stairs" and hitting the door at the bottom of the stairs.

John described the sound as having been "loud and heavy enough to have be an adult" falling down the staircase.

Linda didn't initially connect the sound to the haunting but merely to a housekeeping habit of hers. "Instead of making several trips upstairs in a day, I would put stuff on the stairs and then take it all up [at one time]. When I heard something falling down the stairs, I thought *Oh great, I've got a mess to clean up.* But I opened the door and the stairs were clean. There wasn't even anything there that could have made the sound."

Their reaction to the inexplicable incident showed amazing patience. "We just kind of laughed it off," Linda remembered, and John added with a chuckle, "I told Linda, 'I hope he hurt himself [when he fell]; then he won't be around for a while.'"

As it turned out, John's prediction about the ghost's activity, or lack of it, was correct. There were few signs of the haunting for a while after that. When the phantom pranks resumed, it was with the classic ghostly game of "playing with light switches."

"There was a walk-in closet with a light in our bedroom. We would go to bed and wake up in the middle of the night and the light was on. I'd get up and shut it off," John told me. "Then we'd wake up early in the morning and the light was on again. I'd just go shut it off and go back to bed."

Linda explained that they distinguished between the ghosts. "We feel there were two. The first one actually kind of let us know that it had left. It just walked away one day around 1969. There's a porch on the house with doors at both ends, and one afternoon the inside door opened and closed and then the outside door opened and closed, and

I just got the feeling that [the ghost] was gone. There was a different feeling [in the house]."

Unfortunately, it was not a completely peaceful feeling because there was, of course, still another spectre remaining to haunt them. "It was definitely wanting to let us know that it was around," Linda acknowledged. "Actually the second go-around started when I started reading the Bible really seriously."

By this time John and Linda had started their family. When the remaining spirit began frightening the children, the couple's patience came to an end.

John added, "The bedroom that the kids were using was the room that my mother had blocked off. We had converted it to a bedroom because there was only one bedroom on the main floor and the kids were too young to sleep upstairs. "

When one of their children refused to sleep in that room, John and Linda tried to get him to explain why. "All he would tell us was, 'It's coming for me.' He couldn't describe it. The closest he came was 'It looked like poop,' and that it was in the corner of the room where the heat register was."

By now the family's terror was definitely building. John stated flatly, "We were really concerned about the kids," while Linda described the experience as "like being in a horror novel. The whole feeling was different now. It was ominous."

The ghost began to demand attention by manipulating the basement door.

John explained that there was a door at the top of the stairs leading to the yard. That outside door "would not stay closed even though it was a very, very tight fitting door. It would swell in the rain when it got wet and it was on the north side so it stayed damp for a while. You really had to push that door to get it open. I would bang it, just slam it shut and the next morning it would be open."

Before that problem was solved, the couple had another one. "Furniture began sliding. It went on for maybe 20 minutes. We could hear the furniture sliding right from one side of the room to the other," John explained. At the time, John's brother was living upstairs. John said that one night when they were in bed they heard him rearranging furniture. "We thought that was kind of strange for him to be doing this around midnight but never thought anything more of it and we went to sleep. The next morning when we got up we realized my brother ... wasn't home at all that night."

On other nights, when John's brother *was* home, he "would meditate for a few minutes to relieve stress. Many times [while meditating] he would see something pass between himself and the object that he was focused on."

With this paranormal intruder being so pervasive at night in the house, surely their lives were peaceful outside during the day, I speculated hopefully, but apparently not.

"We were in the garden out in front of the house. A neighbour had a garden there. She was weeding it and we were helping her. She was the one who noticed the face in the window first. She asked who we had upstairs," John said. He added that once their attention was directed to the window, they "could see it too. It was there for a few minutes and then it was gone again."

That sighting didn't really surprise Linda because she frequently "had a feeling of being watched, both in the house and in the yard."

Because they were not able to make out the details of the face, they were never sure if it was the same apparition that was seen twice walking across their yard.

"He was a man in striped coveralls and a hat. He just walked across [the yard] and disappeared. We were in the car coming home. We were coming down the road when we saw this. It wasn't that far away. We thought that someone was maybe breaking in and lifting stuff so we came very quickly into the yard. There was absolutely no place for this man to go. We were in the yard within 30 seconds and he was gone," John told me.

Linda added that there had also been a more recent sighting, probably of the same presence. "Our son saw him another time. He called me one time and said, 'Mom, who's that walking across the yard?' By the time I got to the window there was no one there."

In both sightings, the figure was completely solid and yet just vanished as mysteriously as he had appeared. It might have been that image that captured the attention of John's livestock.

"There would be four, five, six head of cattle and I would be there feeding them. They were just waiting for their feed but they were all looking at exactly the same place with their ears forward. Their heads would move all at the same time as if they were watching something moving across the yard. That happened many times, 20 times, 25 times, 30 times, many times," John said. So many times that "after a while it seemed normal," barely worthy of note.

Despite their patience and acceptance of their difficult circumstances, even this couple had their limit. As would be so with many parents, their children's well being drew the line for them.

"When it was involving the kids we became pretty concerned. That's when we called in the church."

The church member Linda and John contacted "was very knowledgeable. He'd travelled the world, seen voodoo work. He certainly didn't question or doubt us. He was very good. He blessed the house and by about his third visit or so everything quieted down," the pair related.

Sadly, that situation did not end as well for the man who had done the cleansing. "He left the area shortly after that. He had some problems, apparently he lost his voice. It wasn't that long after he blessed this house that he lost his voice. He was going to doctors in Calgary, specialists. They couldn't find a reason. When he blessed the house he asked for protection to the family living in the house. We remember clearly, though, that he did not ask for protection for himself. If he had, would he still be [okay] today?" John asked rhetorically.

The answer is, of course, unknown. The couple is certain, though, that the church member's work succeeded in easing the atmosphere in their house. Despite this, they'd had enough of the stresses of living in that old place.

"From 1970 to 1974 we were saving up enough money to build another house. If we'd had enough money to move [before then] we would have moved in about 1969. We built our new house just across the yard [from the old one]."

When I heard that they built their new house so close to their old one, I asked if their new home was ghost-free. Linda answered, "For the most part yes, but I do occasionally get the feeling that somebody's walked through but not the bad feelings, just more the feeling that somebody's there. There's none of the same nervousness and fear. It's a little eerie but I'm not afraid of it."

John added that since they moved, they have occasionally both heard their names called, both inside and outside the new house, "clearly enough that sometimes we answer back."

And what of the old place? At first, John explained, they tried to turn the liability into an asset by renting it out. The tenants were extremely religious people apparently.

"They were holding church services and prayer meetings there. I think that brought it [the haunting] back around again," John said.

One night the tenants left. "They took off in the middle of the night. They had a garden planted that was well tended. They left all that behind. They had intended to stay. We've never seen them again, we've never heard from them again, they kind of disappeared from our circle."

No one has lived in the century-old structure since.

"After that the house was abandoned and the power was turned off but occasionally we saw lights, mostly in the upstairs bedroom. I would see the lights when it was dark out. I'd say, 'Okay, lights are on, okay, I'm not going into that house,'" John acknowledged.

Phantom lights weren't the only proof that a force was once again at work in the building. "We could hear the sounds of hammering and sawing coming from the abandoned house when we were just standing outside the house we're in now."

Unfortunately, there was one occasion when John had to go back into the old house. "Our water system is still in the old house. It quit working for some reason about 10 o'clock one night so I had to go in. It was a warm winter evening, quiet and dark, with no moon. I took a flashlight and fixed [the problem]. I was standing at the doorway to the kitchen, just looking around when I heard these puppies starting to cry. That really bothered me. I've heard puppies before and I know these were puppies. There were probably three or four of them and they were just crying like when the mother leaves the pups in the box. The second I heard the cries, time seemed to slow down. Everything was happening in slow motion. My body felt weightless, almost like floating. It felt like there were small needles pricking my skin. I remember thinking that if something did come at me from the basement I would not be able to move fast enough to get out of there before it got me. With only a flashlight and a pair of gloves in my hands I had nothing to defend myself with. [After] what seemed like forever, I'm sure only a few seconds, I turned and left," John recalled and then explained the reasons for his actions. "We had heard that things like [the presence] try to lure you. The sound was in the basement. I assumed it was trying to lure me into the basement and I thought *No! I know there's no puppies down there, it's impossible for an animal to get into this house. I hear them but I know they're not there*, so I left.

Linda's sister, who has a history of being psychically sensitive, decided to visit the old place one evening to see if she could determine what was going on.

Linda remembered, "She went over with our nephew but they came back almost right away and said, 'No there's nothing there.' I said, 'What were you doing? Were you checking things out and what not?' She said, 'Yes. We were looking at things.' I said, 'Go back and just sit,' so she went back and just sat. That's when three figures approached from the master bedroom—a woman in white flanked by two dark figures. [My sister] said the two dark forms appeared to be pulling a woman back. My sister couldn't tell if they were human figures. They were very dark and rather vague. My sister left. She came back into the [new] house as white as a sheet of paper. We tried to figure out what it could possibly mean."

The next visitor to the evil old place was the one who caused Linda and John to adamantly rule that no one would ever be allowed to go back into the place.

"She was from Edmonton, a relative of a neighbour. She came with the attitude 'I'm a born-again Christian, nothing can touch me.' She went in and came out and said, 'There's nothing in there.' Then she went back to town to stay at her aunt's. Her aunt was telling me that the woman called her from the bathroom. She was in the bathtub and the more she was washing the redder the water was getting. Her aunt is an old Ukrainian lady from the old country and she just said, 'You should know better. You taunt something like that; it painted you with a red brush.'" Linda concluded her part of that anecdote by explaining "they drained the tub three times before the water would run clear."

The force, however, was apparently not through with its latest visitor even then. The next morning as the woman was driving to Edmonton she stopped to scrape frost off the car's windshield. Unfortunately, she wasn't able to accomplish this as the frost was caught between the two layers of glass that make up all car windows.

John explained, "She couldn't scrape it off. It wasn't on the outside. It wasn't on the inside. It was in the centre, in between the two layers of glass. She ended up driving with her head out the window. She stopped somewhere and had someone look at it and they ascertained that it wasn't frost on the outside. The next morning it was clear."

Since that event the house has stood completely abandoned with just its oddities intact. "In an abandoned house you'll run into spider webs from the ceiling. There were absolutely none there. It was clean. The odd mouse that we did find in there was always mummified, none of them ever rotted. They mummified, just dried up," the owners reported.

By now, the couple has seen some evidence that has made them somewhat optimistic that the ghost may be gone.

John stated, "The house is finally deteriorating now. It's got bugs and mice."

Linda added, "It's doing a more natural thing now."

Perhaps this is because the supernatural elements that once possessed the old building have finally left. For now, the couple who endured so much in the house is only interested in leaving well enough alone. "Unless it becomes a danger," John concluded, "we'll just pretty much just let nature take its course."

Medicine Hat Manifestations

Only very energetic folks get the urge to renovate one home right after another, but Maria and her husband, Rick, of Medicine Hat, certainly fell squarely into that category. As a result, over the past quarter century, they've lived in many houses—several of them haunted.

Their first experience took place in 1978, Maria explained. "Shortly after we moved into a house on 9th Street S.W., I'd smell cigar or pipe smoke every so often."

In addition to the presence of olfactory messages, the ghost even allowed his image to be seen, fleetingly, in the living room, then "when I looked back, no one was there," Maria recalled. Initially, Maria thought that was awfully strange. It wasn't until she "casually asked a neighbour if anyone [had ever] passed away in the house." It didn't really surprise Maria to learn that the original owner, the man who built the house, had died of a heart attack in the living room. His one "big bad habit was that he smoked cigars." Armed with that information, Maria felt quite confident that she had identified her ghost.

Five years later, the family purchased another home in Medicine Hat, this one in the Norwood area, and again intended to renovate. One of the results of their efforts was a spectacular master bedroom suite. That, the couple had planned on. The phantom music, they had not.

"One night I heard organ or piano music around midnight," Maria acknowledged. "Half asleep, I thought a radio or something on the lower level was on. In the dark I went down to check on the kids but heard nothing."

Thinking that her mind was playing tricks on her, Maria began to head back to bed when she heard the music again. As the notes seemed to be coming from a heat register, the woman sensibly presumed that the furnace was somehow implicated. Mustering up her courage, Maria went down into the basement. When she couldn't find any source for the music there, she even went out to the garage, but nothing was out of the ordinary anywhere she looked.

Maria was now curious and, as she had when she lived in her previous home, she began to ask neighbours about the house's former owners. Again her investigation effectively solved the mystery and confirmed that she was living in another haunted house.

Maria explained that she had been told that "the original owners were very musical. The father often played the organ when he could not sleep around midnight." It seems that he'd simply carried his nocturnal habit with him beyond the veil, and Maria and her family were the new audience for his ghostly concerts.

More recently, Maria actually saw an apparition. It came to her in the middle of the night. She was awakened from a sound sleep by the feeling that someone, perhaps one of her children, was about to come into her room. "I lay waiting but heard no sound, no footsteps. Suddenly, in the doorway, a figure of a man, more like a translucent form, went from the doorway, across the foot of my bed, in front of a tall dresser."

The image stopped there. "It turned and looked at me and floated back towards the doorway—then nothing."

Maria sent me a note recently to assure me that all (paranormally) had been quiet in her life recently. Of course, she's not renovating old houses anymore. I suspect that there is a direct connection between those two facts.

Sandstone Spirit

Local legend has it that there is a ghost in the Sandstone Hill area of Calgary. The owner of the haunted house decided to host a Halloween party. Even the weather cooperated with the plans for the spooky party, as thick fog rolled in that night, completing the eerie setting and ensuring that some of the guests stayed the night. Like any sensible group of revelers under the circumstances, the people entertained themselves by telling ghost stories.

Unfortunately, by the time they had themselves good and frightened, the resident ghost began to act up by knocking on the front door. Initially, the guests thought it was just their friends playing tricks, so they searched all around trying to catch the pranksters. The man who knew the house best, however, simply stayed inside. He knew those phantom knocks were always associated with the ghost.

His inside information proved to be correct. The guests weren't able to find anyone near the property nor any sign that anyone had been there. Perhaps that was because by then, the ghost was inside. One of the guests, who was standing in a room with only one door in it, witnessed a human shape walking by him. He was so sure it was a person that he began to talk to it, thinking it was one of the other guests. When he looked up again, however, he realized that he was alone in the room.

The partygoer decided then to leave the gathering. Halloween in a haunted house was, understandably, more than he wanted to handle. Roughly a week later, the man learned that the family who owned the house suspected that the haunting was centred around the door at which the phantom knocking sounds were heard. They took the door down and sold it. It would be interesting to know whether the house is still haunted or whether the ghost went along with the door.

Perhaps, in time, the "rest of the story" will work its way to me, and from there, to a future book.

Laura's Legacy, Part Two

The last story in my book *Canadian Ghost Stories* described a series of terrifying encounters that a former student of mine endured in her teens. When I contacted Laura to let her know that the book had been published and was available, she responded with a cheerful, newsy note—and the additional information that, for a time just recently, she and her husband, Larry, had unwittingly shared their apartment with a ghost.

Albertans expect that the month of January will be cold, but in 1998, it was more frigid than usual. During those bitterly cold weeks, Laura and Larry moved from Edmonton to a suite on the 27th floor of an apartment building in downtown Calgary.

There were many adjustments to be made, not only to the new city, but Larry had started a new job while Laura began an intense college program. For all of us, Laura and Larry included, no matter what sorts of major adjustments we make in our lives, the routine tasks of day-to-day living must still go on. It was while attending to one of these least glamorous chores that Laura thought she'd had a stroke of luck.

"I found four metal candlesticks in our floor's garbage room." Laura wondered why anyone would throw the candlesticks out, and she decided that she would haul the lovely candlesticks home.

Pleased with her find, Laura set her new candlesticks on her dining room table. To add to the decorative effect and to protect the candles from the possibility of melting in the winter sun, Laura placed a planter that was in the shape of a teapot in front of the candlesticks.

One night just a few days later, Larry and Laura headed for bed at their usual hour. They lay in the dark chatting. Then, Laura recalled, "both of us went quiet for a moment. We had become aware of a light that had, apparently, been shining against our [bedroom] wall turning *off*. Since we hadn't been aware the wall had any light shining *on it* in the first place, we wondered how it went off! We turned to one another and started one of those goofy 'Did you see that?' 'Yes, did you?' conversations!"

Unfortunately, Laura was not able to see much humour in the conversation or the situation. She explained, "I had major déjà vu starting—déjà vu that led back 25 years" to her previous experiences with the supernatural.

Despite this ominous feeling, she "tried to forget the 'nonsense' of the odd light. Fortunately, though, I had the sense to write down the date and incident in my planner the next morning."

While jotting the information down, Laura also tried to think of an explanation for the strange occurrence, but she was not successful. "Our suite was on the 27th floor of a downtown apartment building. No buildings were nearby."

Also, being so high up meant that the light could not have been a reflection of either street lamps or car headlights. Things were quiet in the couple's apartment for the next few months when a second mysterious, and apparently sourceless, light shone in the room they used as an office. To make the situation even more confusing, this light appeared during daylight.

Sensitized by the incredible paranormal events she'd been a part of as a youngster, Laura admitted that at that point she "quit trying to explain [the lights]." Her background made her realize there was a spirit present and that with the bizarre light play, "the ghost had said hello."

Laura was determined not to have a repeat of the enigmatic horrors she'd endured 25 years before. She explained, "I decided the ghost or whatever wasn't going to win this time. I was going to have some true peace, lights be damned!"

Wanting to show the presence who was boss, she informed it that she had no time to put up with ghostly shenanigans. "I'm busy with school and plans for the future," she told the spirit.

If, indeed, the entity of light did hear Laura's assertion, it paid no attention to her.

"Remember the teapot [planter]?" Laura asked rhetorically. She was referring, of course, to the one she had used on her dining room table and near which she placed the four candle tapers in her scavenged candlesticks. It seems that one of those candles, only one, had melted and threaded itself, rather grotesquely, through the handle of the teapot planter an inch or so in front of it. "I still haven't figured out how it happened, but it did. We tried to come up with logical explanations and failed pitifully. Out of the four 12" tapered candles only one had melted."

And the results of that melt defied the law of gravity by running horizontally to the teapot and then entangling itself "at an awkward angle," in a seemingly purposeful pattern around the pot's handle. Larry tried to explain the anomaly with "a long geometry theory." Unfortunately, even as he was speaking he knew that his attempt to make sense out of the senseless was failing.

Perhaps because of her experience dealing with a ghost as a teenager, Laura had a slightly more emotional response to the grotesque pattern created by the melting wax melding on to the ceramic pot handle. "I blew a raspberry at the candle and chucked the grossly bent thing in the garbage. I was still determined to get through the haunting as normally as possible."

Laura continued, "Perhaps a few days of quiet ensued—I don't remember. Larry and I have trouble sleeping quite often. He's 6'4" and a quadriplegic. He can often have violent spasms that leave me bruised and jittery. Add to this general life concerns, and we can spend time looking pretty bleary eyed. One night, another concern emerged ... the ghost decided to become a drummer! Larry and I woke up with a start. We turned toward one another and stared, panic etched on each other's faces. Clear as day, except that it was 2 AM, "someone" was drumming a rapid and deliberate beat. We both knew the sound was coming from our living room. We also both knew that someone was beating on our metal-backed dining chairs."

They were terrified. Part of their minds convinced them that someone had broken into their apartment and yet, as Laura pointed out, "most burglars don't drum out a signal. There was an obvious pattern and a definite ferocity to its drumming. Larry later berated himself for not having paid closer attention to the pattern in order to see if it was old Morse code!"

Both Laura and Larry were completely convinced that the "drummer" was in the apartment. Laura acknowledged that given Larry's disability, she was the one who would have to investigate.

"I sneaked down the hall, peeked into the kitchen and dove over to grab a huge knife out the knife block," she remembered. Showing that even abject terror doesn't cause Laura to lose her sense of humour, she added, "Jeepers! Now I'm 'Penny Mason, Private Investigator!' I checked each room, wondering what I would do if I really did find a moron who broke into our suite just to drum at two in the morning. I found nothing disturbed and the door was locked as usual. I went back to bed and, for several hours, lay awake wondering what to do."

The couple mentioned the increasingly strange events occurring in their apartment to very few people but one of those, a workmate of Larry's, "offered 'help' a few days later. He gave us his old Ouija board."

Laura was well experienced with such devices from her previous dealings with spirits. For this reason, when she and Larry sat down at the board, she created a white circle around them. She knew that it would not be safe for either of them to move beyond that encasement "until the session was closed. We had white candles lit around our circle at all times and small containers of salt in between those candles."

After explaining to Larry how the board worked, Laura turned out the electric light and the pair waited. "A moment later gibberish started being spelled out on the board. It started with letters and numbers that didn't make sense. I shrugged and Larry stared. When anyone begins using a spirit board they often suspect that one of the other people is pushing the pointer around the board but ... these things just seem to need no invitation to work."

Soon the gibberish lessened and the board's pointer began to spell out an intelligible message.

"Something identified itself as 'Rose.' [The spirit] had lived and died in the area in the 1950s."

Her death, the spirit indicated through the Ouija board, had been a murder, and her soul still roamed restlessly, unable to find peace. Again Laura's sarcastic sense of humour surfaced when she recalled, "I was tempted to ask if she'd been a drummer but I bit my tongue! Instead, we wished her well and said a polite prayer for her."

After asking if there were any other spirits who wished to come through and finding there weren't, Larry and Laura "closed the session."

From that moment on, the couple's apartment has been ghost free. Possibly, that single session on the board was all it took to send Rose's soul beyond our plane of existence. Laura did acknowledge that they had, by then, replaced the dining room suite that the spirit used to like to drum on and that they no longer place tapers in the candlesticks Laura found when they first moved to the building.

It's possible, Laura suggested, that the spirit left because those two changes effectively took away its toys.

By the time this book is released, Laura and Larry will have moved into their first purchased home. There Laura is planning a similar, but not identical, decorating scheme. "I will once again be setting up our home. The candles will be in the candlesticks [but] I will keep them out of sunny areas so no excuses can occur. If anything [of a paranormal nature] happens I will say a prayer of peace and then [take] the candles back [to] the garbage room where I found them."

Laura closed her correspondence by indicating that she would rather give up the candlesticks, which she is now sure brought the ghostly energy into their apartment, than risk becoming a story in yet another one of my books!

Angry Ashes?

The north end of what is now the central Alberta city of Red Deer was virtually a rural setting in 1950 when Teresa's father began construction of what was to become the family home. Compared to the modern conveniences expected, and supplied, in today's new homes, this small residence was positively spartan, not even connected to city water or sewers until the mid-1950s. At the time those services were finally put in place, Teresa explained that her "father added on to the back of the house, doubling its size."

She continued, "When the basement to that part of the house was being dug out, the fellow [doing the digging] found an area of ashes, probably 10 feet [3.5 m] down into the ground. These, of course, were removed with the rest of the dirt to make way for the basement."

How a pile of ashes came to be buried so deep in the ground and why they were found only in one area was a mystery, not only to the workers but also to the family. Despite being troubled by this enigma, progress, and life, moved along—but not smoothly. It was as if the disinterment of the ashes had unleashed a restless and negative force.

"When the water and sewer pipes were being installed along the avenue, my father chose to install the pipes from the street to inside the house by himself. A deep trench was dug from the street to the house. My dad knocked a hole in the basement wall at the front of the house (the original basement)."

Teresa continued, "When my father was pushing the sewer pipe through the hole in the basement wall, the pipe must have hit the propane tank, as the tank was knocked over and the hose knocked off the tank. My mother went to check what the hissing noise was in the basement but could not see anything wrong. She does not have a sense of smell and so did not smell the propane. As she climbed up the stairs, the propane tank blew up and she was badly burned. She spent time in the hospital. The house burned as well and my father had to rebuild it."

If the restless spirit had anything to do with causing the accident, it didn't stop there. As a matter of fact, judging from the activity that was to follow, the fire only served to awaken the spirit's negative strength.

Teresa explained that after the fire, she "became terrified of certain areas of the original basement. The areas were not where the fire started, but deeper into the basement. I was about five years old. I would hide toys, etc., in a 'safe' part of the basement, away from the thing I was afraid of."

Unfortunately for the little girl's peace of mind, her "fear did not go away. It grew."

Even these many years later, Teresa's assertions were dramatic. "I do not believe the fear stemmed from the fire because too many things happened over the following years. The fear I felt in the two [basement] rooms and just outside their entrance was very intense. It was sudden, like the fear you feel when you have just missed being in a car accident. I'd get goosebumps and my heart would pound. I felt like I was being watched. I felt that fear into my 30s. I finally felt more at ease when I accepted that whatever I was afraid of would not hurt me and really just wanted me out of its space."

Considering all the inexplicable events that transpired in the haunted house that was Teresa's family home, it's no wonder she remained uncomfortable for so long.

In Teresa's detailed accounting she explained that "on Christmas day when I was approximately 11 years old, my cousin and I were in the basement playing. When we went by the entrance to the two rooms I was afraid of, one of the shotguns in my dad's gun rack lifted out of the rack, to the front of the rack, and then back into the rack. There were other guns in the rack but they did not move. I thought it was my brother hiding behind the curtain that was used as a door to the two rooms, but when I went upstairs and asked our mother, I found out my brother was at his friend's house. No one was in the basement except my cousin and me." Teresa added a most understandable comment—that her cousin "was afraid of our basement after that."

As the ghost may have been instrumental in the fire that burned the house down and injured Teresa's mother, it's no wonder that the girls were wary when they saw potentially lethal firearms move about operated by an invisible force.

The family was not always afraid of the haunting, though, as demonstrated in this next anecdote which Teresa described.

"My parents bought a gas dryer. It would turn on and off by itself, no one would be in the basement. If company was in the house and the dryer turned on, [my parents] would say, 'Oh, that's just Henry [the ghost] turning on the dryer.' "

Teresa seemed puzzled by her parents' attitude to this particular ghostly trick. She revealed, "They were amused with the dryer." Perhaps, however, their tolerance was higher than hers because, as far as she was aware, her "parents never had any strange experiences in the basement."

The other possible reason for the parents' greater acceptance of the paranormal activity might be that they were simply less aware of it. It is widely believed that youngsters are more likely to experience the supernatural than are adults. The children's greater sensitivity may have been a factor in this north Red Deer home because Teresa's brother told her that when "he was about 13, he … saw a solid blue line, similar to lightning, shoot from one end wall of the basement to the other end wall. This happened in the area just outside of the two rooms. The same area where my cousin and I saw the gun move."

In case I might have been thinking that he had merely seen something emanating from the outside, Teresa added, "There were no windows in either room."

As the years went by, Teresa grew to be an adult and to have a child of her own. It was through her son that she became convinced that an extraordinary force was at work in her parents' home.

"My son, when he was about two to three years old, would roll toys down the basement stairs, then play with them at the bottom of the stairs. One evening he came screaming up the stairs, 'The fire alarm moved, the fire alarm moved.' He was terrified. He had never heard any stories about things happening in the basement. His fear was real. I do believe my son saw something abnormal happen in the basement that terrified him. He was too terrified to have made it up."

Here again, the theory about the enhanced sensitivity of children might be a factor.

As with many true ghost stories, there is no real conclusion to this strange tale—not a satisfying one, anyway. Teresa indicated, "My mother sold the house after my father died."

Teresa did confirm that the "experiences … in that house made me aware that a lot of things happen that I cannot explain. I do not know whether the ashes found while digging the new basement had anything to do with whatever was in the old part of the basement; however, I never had that fear before then. I do not know if the hose coming off the propane tank and causing an explosion was in any way related to whatever was in the basement. Perhaps the dryer turning on and off was a fault in its wiring. I do know, however, that what I felt and saw cannot be explained. Nor can what my brother or cousin saw.

Although she has never inquired, Teresa acknowledges, "I often wonder whether the new residents have had any strange experiences." Perhaps by today, the anger in the force disturbed when those ashes were removed nearly half a century ago has dissipated and the resident spirit is at peace.

George and Alice

Many people who share their home with a ghost soon come to give their entity a name. I find this phenomenon quite intriguing. It seems to me to indicate that the warm-blooded residents not only have a sense of whether the spirit is male or female, but also believe that the ghost deserves the respect accorded any other member of their household. Oddly, "George" seems to be the single most popular name chosen.

The ghostly George in this story is certainly an active fellow. Alice, his long-standing corporeal roommate, asked that I protect her anonymity in this book by using only an altered version of her first name. After you have read of Alice's adventures with her ghost you will probably understand, as I did, the reasoning behind her request. After all, a resident spirit can affect a home's real estate value.

The haunting began in a particularly scary way. Alice related the initial incident as follows: "One night, I was alone in the house (or so I thought) and was in a dead sleep, when I heard my name called several times. I sat upright. It seemed so real that I went from room to room to see if anyone was there, yet I found no one. I recalled that the voice was as clear as could be and I definitely heard my name called, but [I] didn't know whether the voice was feminine or masculine."

Although she suspected that the voice had called out to her from "beyond the veil," Alice didn't know at the time that the phantom voice belonged to a male ghost she would come to call "George." She also had no idea that calling out her name was only the first ability George would display.

Like many modern-day phantoms, the spectre loved to tinker with things electrical. The television set was one of his favourite toys. Late at night, when the earthly beings staying at the house had been fast asleep for hours, the spirit liked to draw attention to himself by turning on the TV. Worse, he did not respect people's television viewing preferences. Earlier in the evenings, if someone was enjoying a show, the ghost would occasionally turn the channel to another station or turn the TV off entirely.

George's ghostly antics seemed to run in sets. He apparently tired of playing with the television and stopped those hijinks as quickly as he had begun them months before. Next, he started toying with the light switches in the house. He would randomly go about the house turning lights on and off. If there was a pattern or purpose to this activity, it escaped the home's living resident and guests.

Alice kept birds as pets and, like many small animals exposed to supernatural phenomena, these caged birds reacted dramatically to the unseen presence. Occasionally, when all was apparently quiet in the house, the birds would suddenly flap their wings in a vain attempt to fly away from something that had startled them.

The spirit also caused hanging flowerpots to sway back and forth when all was still around them. These instances are not terribly surprising in that they are classic signs of a haunted house. What is, however, always surprising to me under these circumstances is the matter-of-fact acceptance with which the homeowners acknowledge their resident phantom.

"We don't let these things bother us. We just say, 'George has been around again,'" Alice concluded calmly.

And so, as far as we know, somewhere in the southwestern quadrant of Calgary, a phantom named George continues to share a home with a woman named Alice and her family of people and birds.

Whirlwind Visit

Years ago, Kim and her husband, Garry, purchased a small home in an older section of the city of Edmonton. The newlyweds were very excited about beginning their lives together. They bought a house from an elderly couple—the wife was 89 and the husband was 95—who had happily lived in the little house all their married lives. They were delighted to hear that Kim and Garry were not only eager to start a family, but also planned to keep the older couple's beloved garden.

With two such agreeable parties, a deal was soon struck. The legalities were carried out and just weeks later Kim and Garry began settling into their little "doll's house." The process went well and for several years the young couple lived happily and uneventfully in their quaint home. As planned, they started their family and although some people had warned them that they might find the place too small, the new parents found it just right—absolutely comfortable in all ways and everything they needed.

One evening a few years later, after the children were in bed, Kim and Garry were sitting quietly in the living room enjoying a visit with one another.

Did the previous owner of Kim and Garry's bungalow revisit his treasured home at the time of his death?

"It was a very calm evening," Kim explained before adding for emphasis, "that is to say there was absolutely no wind."

Despite this tranquillity, "suddenly a huge gust of wind went right through the house. It was so strong that it lifted the attic door up and down and made a terrible noise."

Badly startled by the noisy, unexpected occurrence, both Kim and Garry leapt from their seats and began to search throughout the house. Part of Kim's great concern was that, as they'd lived there for some years by then, they'd also lived through some pretty severe storms in the house and yet nothing like what they'd just experienced had ever happened "during any storm or windy day."

After spending a great deal of time checking the house over and not finding anything out of the ordinary, they returned to the living room. In order to ease the tension they both felt, they began joking a bit about their experience. "Maybe the former owner of the home came back to haunt us," one suggested to the other with a giggle.

The next morning over breakfast, as Garry was reading the newspaper, he suddenly gasped. The night before, at almost the moment of the strange event in their home, the former owner of the house had died.

Coincidence? Kim thinks not, as "the attic door has never been lifted [off like that] since. I think he was just coming to check on the house that he and his wife had lived in for so many years."

Just as it was in the peaceful years Kim and Garry spent in that house before the whirlwind's visit, their home has been entirely free of any anomalies ever since.

"Is That You, Robert?"

Kim and Garry's house is not the only one I've been told of that had a one-time visit from its deceased previous owner. In 1940, Robert Staysko was a lad of 15, living with his parents in a two-storey home in the southeast quadrant of Medicine Hat. The bedrooms were on the second level, with Robert's room affording a clear view of the upper hallway and the top of the staircase.

"The stairs were solid and never creaked," Mr. Staysko explained to me in a detailed letter.

The Stayskos knew only a bit about the history of the house. Robert noted, "We had been advised by our neighbours that an elderly gentleman had died in the home years before. The death had occurred in the room I used as my bedroom. My bed was positioned in such a way that if I raised my head, I looked straight through the hallway to the top of the stairs."

Robert Staysko continued by describing the evening the phantom footfalls were heard. "It happened in January. My father was a Canadian Pacific Railway locomotive engineer … thus my mother and I were often alone during the night. As I recall, it was a cool night, bathed in bright moonlight. At about two in the morning, something woke me. As I lay completely still, I heard a step creak somewhere down the flight. This was followed by a second creak, and slowly step after step creaked, with each creak obviously moving up the stairs as the noises came closer."

By now, Robert was not only awake but also very frightened by what he could hear and yet not see. "I lay completely still covered with goosebumps and, as a loud creak reached what I assumed was the top step, I realized that I had to do something. I sat up in bed. As I sat staring at the top of the stairs, expecting to see something enter the hallway, my mother called out, "Is that you Robert?"

"No," I answered.

"Did you just come up from downstairs?" she asked.

Rather than reply to his mother's second query, Robert summoned his young courage and "walked over to the top of the stairs, turned the light on, looked down the stairs" and saw "nothing."

"I spent the next hour comforting a worried mother. And, strangely, as long as my parents lived in that house, the incident never happened again."

Perhaps, as in the previous story, the former owner was content just to have had one last visit to his old home.

Water, Water Everywhere

It is amazing to me how often malfunctioning clocks are associated with a ghostly presence. Rae wrote to me of the strange haunting in a Cold Lake apartment she rented from April 1997 to August 1997.

Rae's awareness of something supernatural in the apartment began with "the bathroom door swinging open and shut while I was bathing, the scent of lilacs in the apartment on occasion, the phone ringing and then the ringing suddenly cut off—just little things."

Those rather eerie events might have been tolerable, but what was to follow went well beyond that level.

"We had been out one night and the next morning, when I awoke, I went to the kitchen to make coffee. Coming into the kitchen, I smashed my ankle into the oven door, which was open. Not thinking, I just grabbed the door to close it and, with half a brain, noticed that it was really heavy," Rae recalled.

Her realization came just a second too late. The narrow oven door had somehow become filled with a lot of water, seemingly through two holes at the top of the door. Of course, when Rae put the door upright to close it, the water splashed up and out of the two small holes and trickled down to the floor.

Suspicious that her roommate had something to do with this strange incident, she woke him up. "He came into the kitchen to see" what Rae had been referring to.

"We both smelled the liquid—it was water, but at the top of the door were only two small holes and there were no water marks on the ceiling or on the walls anywhere ... [there was] no discernible way for the water to arrive in the oven door." Even after discussing the oddity with each other, Rae and her friend were not able to explain the bizarre event.

She continued, "Then the clock started freaking out. We would be sitting, well, basically anywhere, and all of a sudden [we would] hear a grinding noise. We would look at the clock and the hands would be spinning—the hour, the minute and the second hands. We would gain about three to eight hours at a time."

The clock did not act like this only once. Rae recalled "sitting at the table eating supper and hearing the noise." They looked up and saw "the clock moving—all the hands at once, spinning hard, like in some kind of cheap horror movie." Not surprisingly, the couple found the strange activity unnerving. "It was enough to move us outside" and to totally deprive them of their appetites for eating.

"The clock thing happened enough" that they "finally got used to it." That was a good thing, for there was more bizarre ghostly behaviour to come. The buzzer that signalled a visitor's arrival at their building's front door was the next device to be affected.

"The security buzzer—either he [Rae's roommate] would hear it go off or I would, but even if we were sitting beside each other on the couch, neither of us would hear it at the same time. We would be watching television and all of a sudden he would jump up and go to the door. He had heard the buzzer but I hadn't—or vice versa."

This active entity was definitely an attention-getter. "I had a rickety computer desk. If you wanted to pull the keyboard shelf out you had to go at an angle and pull very slowly with your knee under it, just in case. Anyway, about two months after the oven door incident I woke up, went to the living room, and slammed into the keyboard shelf. I stopped and looked at it. It was kind of quivering. I looked closer. The keyboard was full of water. All the keys were floating. We never left the shelf out at night; the apartment was too small and to maneuver around it at night was too difficult."

Despite the apparent impossibility, this strange episode had, undeniably, happened, and Rae had to attend to the problem. "When I went to drain all the water out of the keyboard, I found there were four cupfuls in it. Way too much for the keyboard to hold."

Rae's tolerance for living in a haunted apartment had come to an end. She made arrangements to move, but first she did a bit of investigating. The curious woman discovered that the man who'd lived in the apartment immediately before her had died in the hospital. He'd been "a very nice man, by all accounts." As "there was never anything sinister about any of the occurrences," Rae presumed that he had simply come back, in death, to live in his former apartment and didn't want to share it with anyone.

Phantom in Firkins House

Fort Edmonton, located on the North Saskatchewan River bank in Alberta's capital city, is a museum of living history. It is a fascinating place to explore our province's past, especially if you are a ghost hunter, for many of the buildings on the site are haunted. One of the most haunted houses at Fort Edmonton is the Firkins House, named after the home's original owner, Dr. Ashley Firkins, a dentist. I have written about the ghostly activity in this house in my previous Alberta book, *More Ghost Stories of Alberta*, but, since the publication of that anthology in 1996, the Firkins house has been the site of so many new unexplainable occurrences that an update is needed.

The home was built in 1911 on Saskatchewan Drive near the University of Alberta. Over all the years that the storey-and-a-half residence stood on that site, it was owned and lived in by a series of five families. Amazingly, none of them ever modernized any part of the place. The couple who owned the house in the early 1990s decided that, although they loved the location, they could no longer live with the challenges presented by the old house. Rather than tear the place down, however, the family offered it to the city for use in Fort Edmonton Park, where its unrenovated state would be cherished.

Before the painstaking procedure of moving the house began, the owners explained to the staff at the park that the place was haunted. They felt there was a chance that the ghost would go along when the house was moved

Soldiers' efforts to restore the Firkins House were often thwarted by the resident ghost.

rather than stay behind with the family in their new home. As noted in my previous book, it wasn't long before the ghost made it clear that he wanted to stay with his former home.

Since that time, however, workers from Canadian Forces Base Edmonton who volunteered their time and talents to refurbish the residence have documented many new ghostly activities. When the work was ongoing, a heavy old heating radiator simply tipped over, apparently by itself. No one was near it at the time and no (earthly) reason has ever been found for the strange "accident."

When no one was either inside or even nearby outside the house, an upstairs window that had been nailed into its frame mysteriously fell. It was found lying on the hard ground 6 metres below without even one of the four panes broken. No one has ever been able to explain how any part of that event might have been possible.

While there were workers in the house, strange noises were often heard coming from unoccupied parts of the building. The smell of lilacs frequently wafted through one bedroom although it's *highly* unlikely that any of the soldiers on the job would've been wearing such a fragrance!

The most frustrating practical joke that the ghost liked to play was to move the workers' tools around. Just when a soldier would need his hammer or chisel, it would not be where he last put it. Searching the place never did any good. The crew soon learned that whatever was missing would show up again eventually, likely somewhere else in the house.

None of those assigned to the tasks in the house liked to be the last person to leave after a shift. Everyone who had that dubious honour reported that they felt uncomfortable, as though there was an invisible presence nearby. Most concluded that the reason for this feeling was simple—someone, an invisible someone, *was* watching them.

An electrician who was working alone in the house admitted that ever since the day dirt and debris fell on him from "nowhere," he always had goosebumps whenever he was near the Firkins House.

Fort Edmonton Park hosts an annual Halloween celebration. The haunted home is, understandably, an important stop on the tour, but it is also open for display during the park's regular hours. If you visit, do stop to explore the Firkins House. When you're coming down the stairway from the second storey where the bedrooms are, though, please hang on to the handrail. That's where the presence once gave a ghostly shove to one of the home's former occupants.

Although I don't have confirmed information about other buildings at Fort Edmonton, I'm sure there must be more that are haunted. Simply asking one or two of the interpreters, all dressed in period clothing, may net additional information and enhance your day of exploring history and of ghost hunting.

Man in Black

Although Sandy Morris was candid when sharing her experiences with me, it was evident by the tension in her voice that the retelling was extremely difficult for her emotionally. When I learned that her paranormal encounter was with the entity known variously as the Grim Reaper or the Angel of Death and that the encounter was followed almost immediately by a near-death experience, I fully appreciated the depth of her reaction.

Sandy began to recount her terrifying experiences this way: "Late one evening in June of 1999, I was putting the finishing touches on the kitchen cleanup in my home. My husband had gone to bed quite a while earlier."

As the woman worked away in her kitchen, her mind drifted until she "noticed a sound—or was it a movement—in the living room adjacent to the kitchen area."

Sandy looked into the room where she'd sensed the disturbance. It was "dimly lit from the light flowing from the kitchen and dining room area. There was a treadmill in the main entryway at the far end of the living room. When I looked in *that* direction, I noticed a man coming ... *through* the treadmill."

As the horrified woman watched, the entity "crossed in front of the multi-glassed door that led into the study and proceeded down the hall. Its shoulders were hunched and it walked with a trudging gait. At first, I thought that my husband must have gotten up and gone to the front coat closet for some reason. Then I really started to think about what it was I had seen. The man was obviously older than my husband and was not multi-dimensional in appearance. To the contrary, it appeared that he was made out of black construction paper, being flat in appearance."

Her senses heightened, Sandy recalled that she "studied the image's profile. It was one that I shall never forget. He did not look my way, just trudged on by." Desperately wanting to disbelieve her eyes, Sandy ran to check on her husband. She found him just as she'd expected he would be, fast asleep in their bed. "So, who had I seen in my house?" the woman asked rhetorically. In an effort to put the distressing incident out of her mind, Sandy prepared for bed and, moments later, joined her husband.

"The next morning, I got up and had my usual shower. It was about 10 AM, less than 12 hours since I had seen the 'black man.' After showering, I went into my bedroom and, when straightening my leg, felt an excruciating pain in it."

The pain that Sandy felt was so severe that she went directly to the hospital to be examined.

"It was discovered that I had ruptured my calf muscle. I spent weeks fighting extreme pain, taking painkillers and going from doctor to specialist. One evening, about six weeks later, my husband and I went to the neighbours' for dinner. With coaxing, I had two glasses of homemade wine with dinner. As I was sitting there, I felt an excruciating pain go into my shoulder and side."

Sandy's symptoms brought what had been a pleasant evening to a sudden halt and, although she endured the agony for a few more days, Sandy was eventually hospitalized. "A few days later, it was revealed that my leg had developed blood clots which, these many weeks later, had passed through my heart and into my lungs. Thanks to the two glasses of wine, the blood clots had passed through my heart without lodging. I am very lucky to be alive."

During her recuperation, Sandy had plenty of time on her hands and, among other topics, she began to think back to the image of the "black man" that she had seen "a mere 10 or 11 hours before the start" of the events that seriously threatened to take her life.

"At one point, before hospitalization, I thought that maybe he had come to direct me to the world beyond life," Sandy explained. "It frightened me terribly. I was not ready to die! Was he sent to warn me that death was near? I guess I'll never know for sure, but I also know that there is a dimension in this world that we, as living human beings, don't quite understand."

The effect that Sandy's visit from the Grim Reaper had on her psyche was profound. She concluded by explaining that "we who experience things like this carry them on our shoulders, usually alone, for fear of being ridiculed. Discussing these occurrences with other people helps us to deal with these unknown factors. They are very difficult to carry alone."

Thankfully, Death has not revisited Sandy. And, hopefully, as she has now shared her story, she no longer shoulders her burden alone.

"White Lady"

Fort Macleod, near Lethbridge and on the Oldman River, is a pretty little town with a dramatic past that seems to have haunted its present. The Empress Theatre (see *More Ghost Stories of Alberta*) on Main Street in Fort Macleod is not only the oldest functioning theatre in western Canada but is also one of the most haunted.

In addition, legend has it that if the climatic conditions are right, a retrocognitive image appears. A North-West Mounted Police fort originally stood on Fort Macleod-area land that is now a golf course. It was at that fort, more than a hundred years ago, that two men were unjustly hanged. The injustice apparently left the surrounding psychic landscape haunted. Joe Jordan, a man familiar with the course, reports that in the early morning mists it is sometimes possible to see "what looked like two figures 'hanging' over … the second tee box."

As well, aside from the following graphic story, there is at least one haunted house in the town. In the early 1990s, while I was visiting Lethbridge and giving a reading of ghost stories, a woman approached me with a detailed accounting of the ghostly activities in her Fort Macleod home. Disappointingly, I've failed in all my attempts to make contact with that woman since.

The following story, about a different haunted house in the southern Alberta town, is so rich in specifics and has been so carefully documented by the house's former resident that I feel it almost makes up for that previous loss.

This detailed accounting came to me in the form of a long, typed letter. In the opening paragraph, the writer asked that I reveal neither her name nor the address of the house. As confidentiality is something I strive always to respect, I shall refer to my correspondent as Kate.

Many decades ago, when the house was initially built, it consisted of only a kitchen, living room and two bedrooms. Over the years it was renovated and added on to until it had a total of three bedrooms, a dining room, a family room, a new living room and a bathroom large enough to also function as a laundry room.

Kate's parents owned the house in 1966, when, as a young widow with three sons to raise, Kate moved into it.

"The first thing that happened which we couldn't explain was when my mother and I were babysitting my niece who was just beginning to talk a little. I had just put her down for a nap in [the corner] bedroom," Kate recalled before adding that this particular bedroom had an "old-fashioned closet built in it."

"I know [the baby] was asleep because I had stayed with her until she was sound asleep. Then, I went into the kitchen to start on a chore of some kind and in no more than five to ten minutes, my niece screamed. I rushed into the bedroom where she was crying hysterically, sitting upright and pointing to the corner where the closet was. She kept saying 'white lady, white lady.' I settled her down, again waited until she was sound asleep and went back to the kitchen. Again she screamed and it was a repeat of the whole scene. This time I brought her out and settled her down in [another] bedroom. She slept there for a good two hours."

What the child had seen that afternoon forever remains a mystery because Kate's niece was "too young to explain what she meant by 'white lady.' Whether it was the apparition's pallor or clothes we don't know."

Word of this sighting spread and "the son of the man who built this house … came, with his wife, to talk to me about the goings-on here. He explained that … his grandmother had lived with them. She had always worn a large white apron that almost entirely covered her clothes."

The man added that his grandmother had died in one of the two original bedrooms of the house.

During the same time period, Kate's sons, who all slept in the bedroom closest to the basement staircase, were also frightened by ghostly activity.

"They did not tell me until years later that they would regularly hear footsteps come up the stairs, [then hear] the [basement] door open and close, then the footsteps would continue into the dining room and stop just before entering the living room," Kate explained, adding that the footsteps would never be heard going in the reverse direction. The route these phantom footsteps followed was through the original part of the house.

Many years later when Kate's sons were grown, she experienced more ghostly happenings in the house. One day, when Kate was in the basement of the house gathering jars for canning, she "heard the outside door open and close, then footsteps like [the sound of] someone wearing soft leather shoes walk across the kitchen to where the sink was—right opposite the basement door. I yelled that I would be right up. I came upstairs fully expecting to find my daughter-in-law, who lived next door to us, to be waiting as I hadn't heard anyone go out. But there was no one there. I later asked my daughter-in-law what she had wanted, but she said that she hadn't been there."

Flesh-and-blood beings weren't even accorded any privacy in the bathroom. "For the longest time, every time I would get up in the morning and go to the bathroom to get dressed and cleaned up, there was a jiggling at the door as if someone was trying to get in. The first few times this happened, I called out that I would be right out. One time I even opened the door, thinking that [someone] needed to get in, but there was no one there. After that I just ignored it, but a lot of times I had the uncomfortable feeling that someone was watching me," the long-suffering woman wrote.

Kate wasn't the only one to suffer that humiliating experience. Her sister-in-law "said on several occasions while she was in the bathroom, she had heard the back door open and close and footsteps come into the kitchen but never go back out, so, when she came out of the bathroom she fully expected to find my brother waiting. But no one was ever there."

During a time when Kate and her children had moved to Lethbridge, they periodically returned to the old house to visit with Kate's parents. "My boys had to sleep on a sofa-bed in the living room and they told me that pretty well every night they would hear these footsteps on the stairs [that would] stop at the living room doorway. They said they were so scared that they would hide under the covers till they could fall asleep."

Soon Kate moved back to the house in Fort Macleod and right back into the haunting. "I was in the habit of reading in bed before going to sleep, always with the door shut [and chain locked]. One night there was no noise of any kind but something made me look up at the door. It had quietly opened to the full length of the chain. I puzzled about this for a while as this was in winter with absolutely no draft source."

Then, showing amazing acceptance of her strange situation, Kate merely shrugged and turned her attention back to her book. "A few minutes later something again made me look at the door. It had quietly shut again."

By 1979, Kate had remarried and, in doing so, had taken on parenting duties to a 12-year-old stepdaughter. The girl slept in the bedroom that Kate's boys had shared many years before. In an attempt to protect the child from fright, the adults and the girl's three stepbrothers deliberately withheld all the information about the haunting from her. Despite this, "she was terrified when she was supposed to go to bed as, most nights, she would hear footsteps on the stairs continuing into the dining room. She also said that her closet door would open and close as if someone was coming into her room from there."

While phantom footsteps and doors opening and closing had become almost routine to the members of this haunted household, a visitor experienced a different twist on that theme. The guest and her friend were sleeping on the sofa-bed in the living room when the guest "was wakened by a knock at the outside door. The door opened and closed then someone very urgently said for her to hurry and get dressed, that her friend was ready and waiting to go. She was a bit groggy but got dressed. She was just putting on her shoes when she happened to glance to the other side of the bed and her friend was lying there sound asleep."

No part of that mystery was ever solved.

Kate maintained in her letter to me that through all the 31 years she lived in, or visited at, the old house, she "never felt threatened or afraid." Even so, this is one of the few ghost stories I have encountered in which people have been inexplicably harmed.

"I wish I could say that nobody was ever hurt but I had occasion to go to Brooks, where my eldest son lived, for the weekend. When I returned home my husband asked me to check his back. He said that [in the middle of the night] he had turned over to the other side of the bed and experienced a horrible burning pain on his back. This bothered him for the rest of that night and was still uncomfortable the next day when I got home. In fact, it continued to be quite painful until it healed up. I checked it and right on the bottom of his shoulder blade, toward the centre of his back, where he couldn't possibly reach, there were three very angry red scratch marks. They were about 4 inches long [6 centimetres] with a kind of zippery effect. They were side by side and slightly curved. They looked like the claw marks of an animal," Kate explained, before adding simply, "we have no pets."

Sadly, Kate's husband was not the only one to suffer such wounds. "My second oldest son was staying with us for a bit right around this time and was using another bedroom. He woke up one night with the same scratch marks on his mid-thigh. He, too, said they burned like fire. They took quite some time to heal."

Not too long after those mysterious injuries occurred, Kate and her husband were ready to sell the house and move on. Even so, the place stayed in the family, for they sold it to Kate's youngest son, but not before arrangements were made to have a minister say a prayer and bless the house. That ritual seemed to finally put an end to the haunting. The ghost, however, may have saved one final trick as a farewell to Kate.

"The first night we spent in this [new] house, I hadn't unpacked anything yet, just set up the bed and [then we] went to sleep. Suddenly we were both awakened by a loud noise, as though tin baking pans had crashed to the floor in the kitchen."

Since that strange bit of possible housewarming activity, however, Kate and her family are all, at last, most contentedly living in ghost-free peace.

A Phantom
Named Fiona

A Scottish couple that lived in the Palliser neighbourhood of Calgary left an interesting legacy. Sadly, the wife, Fiona, developed cancer and died shortly after the diagnosis. As was her wish, though, when she passed to the other side, she was not in the hospital surrounded by strangers but in her beloved house with her loyal husband, John, at her side.

Not long after Fiona's death, John decided that there was no longer anything tying him to Canada. He wanted to sell everything but his most personal possessions and move to his native country but was overwhelmed by the prospect of organizing and carrying out the move. So, for six months, he stayed, miserably, in his Calgary home.

One afternoon, while John was taking a nap, his long-deceased mother appeared to him in a dream. She assured him that a friend would help him and that all would be well. Not long after that visitation, John's neighbour, whom we'll call Stan, came to him with a business proposition. Stan's daughter had just recently married and the newlyweds were looking for a home.

"What would you think if I gave you a down payment for the house and then my daughter and son-in-law took over the mortgage payments?" Stan asked John.

The widowed man was delighted. Not only would this relieve him of the complications inherent in a less friendly sort of real estate transaction but, as he and Fiona had known Stan's daughter, he also felt he was leaving the old place in good hands. And so it was that Wendy and Warren (pseudonyms) came to their first home—a fully furnished house complete with two cars. There was even food in the kitchen cupboards. Or, as Warren's mother told me, "everything was the way the wife had left it" at her death.

John moved back to Scotland and no one ever heard from him again. The young couple moved in and, in keeping with the agreement, continued to make the mortgage payments. Soon after, although they didn't recognize it as such at first, Wendy and Warren began to see evidence that the ghost of the former owner's wife had not gone back to the British Isles with him.

One of the first signs that something unusual was going on was that the couple would frequently see lights on that should not have been on. At first they blamed each other, to the point that the matter was beginning to become a factor in the relationship.

"You've left the light on in the kitchen again," the young husband accused his wife, who was in the basement at the time. "No, I turned it off when I came downstairs," she maintained. To make matters even more puzzling, the two were alone in the house, or at least, they thought they were. Some hours later, Warren found the light in the spare bedroom was turned on, but, as with the previous incident, Wendy was positive that she had turned it off when she left that room.

That night, the two were in bed reading when, once again, the light in the spare bedroom came on. Not knowing what else to do, Warren simply got up and turned the light off again.

By now the newlyweds were becoming convinced that they had taken over much more than just a furnished house and mortgage payments—they were quite sure they also had a ghost. And, in all likelihood, they were right.

One evening when they were watching television they both heard the toilet flush. Together they rushed up the stairs and into the bathroom. The toilet was, by then, refilling. It was then that they finally acknowledged Fiona's lingering presence. The realization actually made living in the haunted house easier, for then, if something was not as it should have been, they would just tell themselves that Fiona was up to her tricks again. Because Wendy had known the woman in life, she certainly didn't fear her in the afterlife.

This was not to say that the ghost always made the couple's life easy because she certainly didn't. One of her most irritating tricks was to rearrange their possessions. The young bride remembered, "I would come and find that my things had been changed around. Fiona obviously didn't like where I put something so she moved it. I'd put it back and then go to work the next day. Sure enough it would be moved by that evening."

Wendy began calling out a greeting to the ghost whenever she came home. As fate would have it, however, just as they became used to their invisible roommate, they lost her. They held a garage sale to clear out all the household effects that had been left to them but that they really didn't want or need. Soon after the garage sale, Warren and Wendy realized that Fiona no longer seemed to be around.

It seemed that once Fiona's possessions were gone, her soul no longer felt attached to her former residence. It would be interesting to know whether the woman's spirit went with one of her possessions sold at the sale, joined her husband back in Scotland or simply passed on to her final reward.

Elderly Entity

For more than half a century, the large, three-storey house perched atop the north bank of the North Saskatchewan River. The view from the south-facing windows was one of the most spectacular in Edmonton. In late spring and throughout the summer, the panorama was the lush green provided by nature and the greenskeepers at Victoria Golf Course. In fall that same scene was ablaze with the deep gold colours of autumn, and when winter came, the breathtaking scenery was blanketed in snow, becoming a winter wonderland.

Despite such beautiful surroundings, the one permanent resident of this old house was heart-wrenchingly sad. We have no way of knowing how long the unhappy entity had been in the house. We only know for sure that by the 1970s, the place was definitely haunted. By that time, the house was no longer a regular family home but a meeting place for the Big Sisters, a community organization that matches girls up with positive role models. When the women who worked for the society, and their "Little Sisters" who were the group's clients, finally saw the ethereal old woman, they were very distressed by her evident sorrow but they were not really surprised by her presence. They'd endured so many inexplicable oddities around the place

Occupants of a house that looked out upon this scene in Edmonton sometimes saw something more mysterious.

that most of them accepted that the house was haunted.

Barb, who was a Little Sister, told me, "I can remember not feeling comfortable entering this house alone. A person would get a real eerie feeling."

Adding to this general feeling of discomfort were some very specific ghostly incidents. Barb explained, "There was a bathroom just off the kitchen. It had only one entrance and no windows that anyone could fit through. The bathroom door had an eyehook lock. On many occasions this bathroom would be found locked from the inside."

The bathroom wasn't the only room that would suddenly and mysteriously become locked. "The office door, right next to the bathroom, had a skeleton key and the door would be locked with the key still inside the room."

The day most memorable for paranormal activities was in the middle of winter. "We had to use the porch entrance [to the house] because the kitchen door was snowed in and frozen shut," Barb recalled.

Once inside the house and enveloped in its welcoming warmth, Barb and the staff members who were with her sat in the living room chatting. All the while they were in clear view of the one functioning door to the house, so they knew no one had come in since they had. Despite this, when they moved into the kitchen, they were upset to see an elderly woman sitting at the kitchen table, "crying uncontrollably," Barb acknowledged. Although they must have wondered how the woman had managed to get into the house, they put their concern for her emotional state first.

As Barb stood by, "one of the staff members sat with the woman and tried to find out what was wrong. She started rubbing the old woman's hands but the more she rubbed them, the drier they became. She asked me to go grab the hand cream that was in the office but I couldn't find it."

The worker left the woman's side for just a moment to join Barb in the office area and to locate the moisturizer. Seconds later, a bottle of lotion in her hand, the worker, followed by Barb, "went back into the kitchen but the old woman was gone."

The sad, elderly lady was not in any physical or emotional condition to have left the house by herself. Even stranger, during the time that Barb and the worker who had been comforting the sad soul had been in the office, "the other girls were there by the only entrance in or out and no one saw her leave."

Terribly concerned and confused, everyone who had been in the house "went outside to see if we could find the woman, but there weren't even any footprints to suggest she had entered or left the place at all."

The distraught image had simply vanished. While this added even a bit more "strangeness" to the old house, most of those who met there felt that they had now seen the ghost whose presence they'd been aware of for so long.

As the house was torn down not long after that sighting, we can only hope that the demolition sent the anguished wraith to a place of contentment.

Evil Echoes

The settlers who came to Alberta were as diverse as the province they came to, so no two pioneer experiences were alike. Many of those who came to settle in the Canadian West did not stay. Some moved on to other areas, others returned to their homeland, leaving nothing behind to prove that they had ever been part of the immigration wave. Others left only echoes, and in the case of the Englishman from whom the immigrant Price family purchased their farm, they were gruesome, ghostly echoes.

In the 1920s, the Prices settled on the haunted rural property near Ponoka. One of the sons was the first to have a paranormal experience in the house. One night the young man was awakened by the sound of tree branches brushing up against the window of his second-floor bedroom and shadows from those branches moving about the walls and ceiling of his room.

The next morning he decided to ensure that the offending tree would never interrupt his sleep again. Armed with an axe, he headed out to chop the tree down. As he rounded the corner of the house, however, Price was most surprised to find that there wasn't a tree anywhere near his bedroom window. Shocked and puzzled, he was grateful, at least, that he hadn't mentioned the disturbances to the other members of his family, who might well have wondered about his mental stability. As it was, the young man simply went on with the other chores he'd planned for the day, which were undoubtedly easier to accomplish than trying to explain, even to himself, the existence of a tree that didn't really exist!

The young man's grandmother had the next phantom encounter. One night as she slept in her main floor bedroom, an invisible force pinned her to the bed. She lay there completely overpowered until an image appeared at the foot of her bed—an image of a young boy dressed in overalls. The spirit of the youth ordered the force to release its hold on the terrified lady. As the ghost child communicated his demand, the pressure on Grandmother Price's body lightened until it released her completely. As it did, the apparition vaporized. Not surprisingly, the woman decided to choose another bedroom. Once she and her eldest son switched rooms, the ghostly encounter never recurred.

Eventually the family decided to move on. They purchased another farm, roughly 15 kilometres from the old one. For security, one of the sons stayed behind one additional night at the old place with only his dog for companionship. The man fell asleep in a bed by the kitchen stove. He woke during the night to see a shadow on the wall—a shadow in the shape of a human. As the man watched the strange sight he heard a loud thump, followed by the sound of something heavy being dragged across the floor. The noise stopped at the door to the cellar.

The man immediately got up to investigate. As soon as he opened the front door, his usually reliable dog, which had been cowering in fear, bolted from the house and was not seen again for two days.

Once the Price family was reunited, they began to share their strange experiences with one another. It was only then, after moving out of it, that they realized they'd been living in a haunted house.

A bit of research into the history of the land they had just moved from told them that the previous owner had been a cruel man who was violent toward his wife and his sons as well. When the boys grew big enough, they moved away, assuring their father that they would come after him if he ever beat their mother again.

With his children gone, the man found it difficult to run the farm, so he sent for an English orphan to come and help him. The boy arrived and began work but disappeared shortly after and was never seen again. About that time the vicious man's wife appeared in town, apparently badly burned. Townsfolk eventually figured that she had been injured while enduring yet another of her husband's beatings. The immigrant lad, who was never seen again, was assumed to have tried to come to the woman's aid but had, the neighbours suspected, been murdered in the process.

The sights and sounds that Price encountered during that last night in the house were ghostly echoes of that fatal altercation. Sounds of the boy's body hitting the floor and being dragged to the cellar for immediate burial had imprinted themselves into the atmosphere of the house. In other words, it had become haunted. After a while it was generally accepted that the apparition the grandmother had seen was the ghost of the murdered boy, once again defending a woman from the cruelty of the home's original owner—even as a ghost.

That haunted rural farmhouse was torn down decades ago. The tale, part of the immigrant family's lore, was incorporated into our province's heritage when it was described by Robert G. Price in the Spring 1982 issue of the magazine *Alberta History*.

Farmhouse Follies

As the wife of an Alberta farmer and the mother of a young family, Luella's moments of leisure were limited, but surely this was one. It was evening, her husband was out, her children safely tucked into bed. The woman reclined on the living room couch, her eyes open, her mind wandering.

Seconds later she was jolted from her reverie when she saw an enormous shadow on the opposite wall. It was the shadow of a person, at least the shape was that of a human figure—a *huge* human figure. Seconds later the silhouette was gone. It had vanished as mysteriously and quickly as it had appeared.

Too startled to be concerned about possible danger, Luella ran to the door of the house and out into the yard, intending to confront what she presumed was a trespasser—but there was nothing to be seen, nothing that could have caused the enormous human-shaped shadow. Still determined to protect her children from any conceivable harm, the frightened woman went back inside to check in there. Her search in the house proved to be as fruitless as her search of the yard. Deeply puzzled by what she'd just experienced, but sure there was nothing else she could do at the moment to solve the mystery, Luella lay back down on the sofa. Despite its disconcerting nature, that incident might in some way have served to prepare the woman for the sourceless shadow's next trick.

The setting for the phantom's second visitation was much the same. It was evening, and Luella's husband was out of the house and her children were asleep. Again, she lay relaxing on the living room couch. This time, however, as she reclined on it, the piece of furniture lifted up from the floor "about 3 inches." The terrified woman managed to climb off the elevated sofa and, as soon as she did, the piece of furniture lowered itself back to the floor.

After standing and staring in disbelief at the couch that had just taken her for an unexpected and unwanted ride, Luella lay back down. No sooner had she managed to relax her tense muscles than an invisible force picked the sofa up again. By the time this had happened a third time, the woman was badly frightened and decided to retreat to what she thought was the security of her bed. Unfortunately, the change of room didn't provide the tranquillity she'd hoped it would. Not only did the bed elevate, just as the couch had, but the enormous shadow that she'd seen in the living room on a previous evening appeared to her again, this time on the bedroom wall.

Luella's daughter, Betty, who related her mother's

paranormal encounters to me, declared that no explanation was ever found for the strange occurrences and that no levitations ever happened again. From then on the family simply accepted that the house was haunted.

Their belief that they lived in a haunted house was soon reaffirmed. Betty set the stage for her description of the events with some clever wording: "Our ghost was very alive on this morning," she stated.

"Mom and Dad were getting ready to do the chores. Before they went out Mom was preparing to build a fire in the stove in the kitchen. [She] had crinkled up newspaper and put it in the stove. She turned ... to pick up some kindling to put in there, but, when she turned around again, she got a big surprise. The paper had straightened out completely, as if it was never touched. There was not a crease in it."

Perhaps the combination of the companionship of her husband and the fact that it was daylight gave Luella confidence, for rather than reacting in fear, Betty's parents both "joked about it, knowing it was the ghost." The joking continued for a moment and the two "started making jokes about other things in the kitchen," Betty recalled. "I suppose they didn't think the ghost would be listening but found out different. Dad made a comment [to the effect that] his boots and the milk pail [might] walk across the floor next. The ghost obliged him."

The couple's joking ceased after that display! Betty remembered, "We didn't stay in that place very long after those incidents."

Betty relayed another compelling story of the ghost in her parents' home. Picture a farmhouse in southern Alberta, "between Taber and Lethbridge," the era, the 1950s. Betty was then a little girl, five or six years old. "I used to spend a lot of time sitting by the kitchen window, just looking out and taking note of everything I could see that was happening outside," Betty recollected.

One of the "happenings" she looked forward to seeing regularly was a family, "a man, a woman, a child and a dog walking down the road past our house." The people's images were clear and solid. There was nothing about the appearance of these folks that would have given the child cause for even a second thought, much less a fright.

Betty remembers being a bit puzzled, therefore, when "on several occasions I had told my mother that these people and their dog were walking down the road past our house but whenever she came to the window to see, she saw nothing."

This pattern continued over a period of time until, as Betty described, "finally, one day my mother did see them." While this confirmed that the child was not imagining things, her mother was not as accepting of the sight as the little girl had been. "They didn't look normal to her," Betty explained.

Not long after, Betty's family moved to a new farm. Their previous house, where the child had spent so many hours happily gazing out the kitchen window and watching the mysterious family and their dog, was torn down. It was then that a bit of the mystery might just have been solved.

Skeletons were found buried under the house's foundation. The remains had apparently been there for some time. Could it be that the images that Betty had routinely watched with such interest and that her mother thought looked odd were the ghosts of the people whose bodies had been disposed of on the property? That's the conclusion that Betty's family came to, especially when they learned that one of the skeletons had been identified as having been that of a little girl.

Another Image in Irma

Erin contacted me after reading one of my previous books about hauntings in our province. She had a lifelong interest in the subject of ghosts, partly because her father passed away when she was a year old. As Erin explained, "I've always been sure that had something to do with it because [the possibility that the souls of the dead can be with us] has just fascinated me."

With that general interest in the paranormal, Erin read *More Ghost Stories of Alberta,* which includes a story about a house in Irma where, in the mid-1970s, a young couple spent a few horrific hours. Those specific events were of great interest to Erin because her mother, Doreen, had been raised in Irma—in a haunted house. After hearing of Doreen's childhood home, Erin and I quickly concluded that it was not the same building, but it was quite a coincidence just the same because, as Erin pointed out, the community of Irma's "not that big."

The young woman began to relate the circumstances of the paranormal experience her mother had as a child. "My grandparents were very, very poor. It was during the Depression; my mother would've been about five years of age. My mother's parents lived in the vicinity of Irma. They needed a house, so her brothers helped my Granddad move a granary that was going to be torn down. They moved it onto this little piece of land. Then they built onto it and that was their house. Even though it wasn't a *house* before, it was certainly a building with quite a bit of history."

The family settled into their new home. Doreen, the youngest of the four children in the family, shared a bed with her sister. "Mom said that my aunt wasn't cuddly at all so she couldn't cuddle up beside her, and Mom had a terrible fear of the dark so there were many nights when she was awake through the whole night because she was terrified. For this reason Mom *absolutely* knows she was awake when this happened."

Doreen had emphasized, "I know this wasn't a dream."

Although Doreen was awake, the incident had all the qualities of a terrible nightmare. Erin relayed her mother's experience this way: "She woke up from a sound sleep and saw something in her peripheral vision. She looked toward it and saw her mother was standing beside the bed with a knife in her hand, staring at her."

If that vision weren't terrifying enough, Doreen's next realization made the situation even more frightening. "She could see right through the image but it was wearing a dress that my grandmother wore at the time and that my Mom was very fond of. For hours, this thing just stood there with the knife poised right at her. Mom knew it wasn't real, but, at the same time, she couldn't understand what on earth it could be. Mom tried to cover her head up and roll over, and every time she looked back there was this thing."

Erin acknowledged that her mother "genuinely loved her Mom and Dad. She was very kind and outgoing. She had no hidden agenda when they lived in this house." Either in spite of, or because of, these facts, Doreen "never told anyone. She often said to me it was the weirdest thing because it never happened to anyone else in the family," and she knew it would "deeply disturb her parents" to hear about it.

Erin wonders, though, if other members of the family had also seen the horrible image at different times. She reminded her mother that there were several incidents recorded in *More Ghost Stories of Alberta* that indicated more than one family member had experienced a ghostly interaction but, at the time, had not spoken of it with anyone else. It was quite possible, therefore, that Doreen was not the only one ever troubled by frightening phantoms in the granary-cum-house.

Erin has theorized to her mother that a supernatural being "wanted to cause trouble for you. It wanted you to go yelling to your Mom saying 'This is what I saw!' and because you didn't, you set it right off guard. It didn't know what to do with you. There was no point in messing with you anymore because it wasn't fun."

Perhaps the being that had taken on Doreen's mother's appearance should have done a little more thorough background check, for Erin stated, "My grandmother was a real English lady, raised by a real English family. She was very gentle and kind, very spiritual all her life. The thought that she would be in this position was absolutely absurd but it disturbed my Mom so. That dress was one that she knew well and recognized. The image didn't just flicker and then wasn't there anymore. It stayed. Something must have taken on the appearance of my grandmother."

What the seemingly evil entity really was, or what it wanted that night has, evermore, remained a mystery.

Scowling Police Presence?

Legend has it that an old house near Calgary's downtown is haunted. As the residence was built circa 1910 on a lot once owned by a captain of the North-West Mounted Police force, some who've come in contact with the phantom feel that his spirit is the resident ghost.

As in many hauntings, the presence kept a fairly low profile until a renovation project was started. Once the overhaul began, the ghost really began to make itself known. The house was extended and a new kitchen was added on. As a group of adults and children watched in horrified amazement, the recently added room broke away from the older part of the building. If you're thinking that it simply slumped because of faulty construction, then you'd be wrong, for the new room did not fall, but, in defiance of the laws of gravity, rose almost half a metre before settling back into place.

Whatever the presence was, it would travel back and

forth between the main house and a two-storey outbuilding on the same lot. The spirit must have been most unhappy about the changes to "his" property because the atmosphere in the buildings became decidedly negative—so much so that the occupants of the house arranged to have the place exorcised. Along with the priest who oversaw the ritual, there were 13 people in the group. The participants formed a circle and tightly held hands. According to those in attendance, as the ceremony began, a spot on the floor in front of them seemed to be the epicentre of the haunting. One woman had to be held in order to keep her from falling face first into the threatening area. That was enough for all involved. They quickly gave up the idea of an exorcism and disbanded. They feared that continuing would cause them to come away with more than just a bad fright and a story to tell their grandchildren!

The ghost has continued to make his presence known. For the most part his phantom hijinks are little more than a nuisance. He's been known to tip over furniture and equipment as well as to hide people's belongings. Occasionally, however, he'll allow himself to be seen, and those who've seen the apparition have been given a real scare. They describe a short, heavy-set bearded man, probably in late middle age. He has an unpleasant look on his face, as though he's displeased with something in his life or, perhaps, his afterlife. The ghost's thick hands clasp a pitchfork. He is dressed in a vest and boots of the style worn one hundred years ago.

Others who've glimpsed the entity haven't seen him quite that clearly, seeing only a sourceless shadow in the shape of a man, but have been equally unnerved by the encounters. These incidents have usually occurred in the basement of the house.

It is suspected that at least three other spirits exist in the 90-year-old house. The phantom cries of a baby are heard occasionally when there are no flesh-and-blood children on the property. When there *are* children visiting the house, they have told various adults that they like playing with the ghost of a little boy in the living room.

The third ghost is that of a young woman, possibly the mother of either the baby or the little boy ghost. She is a decidedly benign presence who never bothers anyone but simply resides in the building.

An investigation into the history of the land and the buildings on it did not reveal that any untimely deaths had occurred there, but that does not rule out the possibility of phantoms there. Maybe the energies of the spirits were attracted to one another or came in on a piece of furniture or building material in the old place. Of course, it's also possible that they have simply found that piece of downtown Calgary real estate to be hauntingly to their liking.

In case you're worried that you might inadvertently buy this house as a residence, we can set your mind at ease. It's long been used for commercial purposes only.

Containing the Entity

Andrea began her note by telling me that she reads my books for comfort! I thought I'd heard everything, both good and bad, in the way of reader responses to my work until that comment arrived in the mail. As I pored over Andrea's letter, though, I began to understand. She explained that since her pre-adolescence, she has had encounters "with the supernatural, more specifically, a poltergeist."

Translated from German, the word "poltergeist" means "noisy ghost." These beings, known for their activity and high energy levels, are usually associated with a person rather than a place. Very often, poltergeists are attracted to adolescents. It is said that the energy emitted by the onslaught of hormones in teenage bodies is a virtual invitation to this sort of entity. Much of Andrea's story fits that description.

She began by explaining that her "mother had the house [in the Blue Quill area of Edmonton] built in 1986. It's such a beautiful house but the minute we moved into it, I hated the place. I didn't want to move in. I couldn't sleep with the lights off. I had to sleep with my sister because of all the things happening. I thought I was going crazy. It was a horrible time."

Andrea provided details to describe the strange haunting. "There was the terrible, terrible hiss—a sharp, cat-like hissing sound. Every night for years before I went to sleep, just as I was dozing off, that horrible hiss would wake me up. I didn't know what it was. Later, 2 to 3 AM, the activity would start. The only way I can describe it is that it seemed like a party was going on downstairs. The activity only escalated from that point on. I began to see things, some [were] so frightening ..."

The personable young woman continued, "One time I saw this little thing, I don't know how to even describe it—like a blob of something black running around the bed. I didn't know what it was, I thought I was going nuts so I put it out of my head, covered myself right up and went to sleep."

When Andrea told her mother about these frightening experiences, the older woman initially didn't believe her. "She blamed it on the fact I was going through puberty." Her mother's opinion was soon to change.

"One night, my mother was sleeping in the den, which was unusual. That night, she heard the same noises that I had been hearing. She woke up with such a start and couldn't go to sleep the rest of the night. A few weeks after that my sister heard the sounds. She heard it a few times, so they started to believe me."

It's a good thing that Andrea had her family's support by then because "the ghost began to haunt around the clock. My mother and sister were convinced that some presence was among us [but] the ghost seemed to prefer me."

That did seem to be the case, but it was a strange sort of preference. "The more I screamed, the more I cried, the more terrified I was of this 'thing,' the more it came to visit me, growing stronger every time." It was as if the entity was feeding off Andrea's terror-filled energy.

"I'd sit in the house and be so sure that someone was staring at me or that someone was around. I'd feel like things were crawling on my skin, like the feeling if a spider's crawling up your leg but all over. It was always around me … I'd hear things in the middle of the night. I'd wake up and I'd hear a party going on downstairs. No one else was up so I'd go out to the hallway and turn the light on. The noises sounded like high-heeled shoes on my kitchen tiles and then the sounds of drawers opening and slamming shut and of utensils going crazy inside them."

Despite all the auditory evidence at these times, Andrea never saw anything to confirm what she was hearing.

Even the daylight hours were not calm. "I remember one time I was doing the dishes. It's a huge kitchen and a two-storey house. I heard someone stomping their feet upstairs and [the footfalls] went from one end of the house to the other, but there are walls separating rooms upstairs where this was happening. There's a bedroom, a bathroom and the master bedroom all in a row. I heard this stomping noise above my head go all the way through the walls to the end of the house and back. I just ran outside, I couldn't take it. I was scared. Others have heard this too."

Others have even seen supernatural beings in Andrea's home. "My aunt came from Poland about three years ago. She went to bed her first night here and came running out in a big horror. We hadn't told her anything about this house because we didn't want to freak her out, but apparently she had seen this white form floating around."

Andrea's pet, a Samoyed dog named Chantelle, was sensitive to the ghost's presence. "She [Chantelle] used to alert me [to the fact] that something was going to happen. [She would begin] whimpering and trying to get outside the house. Sometimes I'd hear her howling downstairs or sometimes she'd come upstairs and just cower." Andrea recalled a particularly painful experience with the phantom:

In my late teens, I was blow-drying my hair in the bathroom. There are two fire alarms [nearby]. One's right by the bathroom and one's at the end of the hall by the den. I had taken a shower about an hour before, but I have really long thick hair so I don't dry it all at once. I heard the fire alarm go off right by the bathroom, and I thought it was my hair dryer that had set it off. It did seem strange, though, as that had never happened before. I went to shut it off but it wouldn't shut off so I started waving a towel over it trying to clear the air. It would not shut off. Then, the second fire alarm started sounding and I went to that one. My ears were just about to burst at this point. I tried to shut the second one off and it wouldn't shut off. I'm fanning these things, finally they both shut off so I walked toward the bathroom again, got halfway there and both of them start up again. I'm doing everything I can to shut these things off because my ears are bothering me so much that I can't think or I would have just gone down to the fuse box and disconnected the power but I couldn't even think of that.

Andrea's anger and frustration at the phantom's hijinks were, understandably, getting the best of her by this time. "Finally I got so frustrated that I knocked the alarms down with a broom handle. Then I took one of the wires off to disconnect it but even that didn't help. First one starts going, then the other starts going. I don't know how this is happening because they're disconnected by now. (One of them is permanently broken. I knocked it so hard it can never be fixed.)"

Despite having destroyed the devices to the point where they should not have been able to function any longer, Andrea recalled that the noise "went on for 45 minutes. It was like someone was laughing at me. Someone was having a really good time. Such a good practical joke. There was nothing in the house to set the fire alarms off, no one smokes in this house. It never happened before or again.

"It [the poltergeist] even began presenting itself to friends and one of our neighbours. To this day, a friend of mine will not enter the house because of an experience we had when we were about 13 years old. So many horrible images and activities went on for years until my neighbour blessed and cleansed the house in 1998."

The neighbour's attempt to expel the spirit was, apparently, at least partially successful, for Andrea explained that "the activity has calmed down [although] I still experience things I would rather do without, and if there's a negative person in the house, he or she will hear it [the poltergeist]."

After the cleansing ritual had been completed, the woman who performed the blessing spoke to Andrea. "She came out pale and shaking. She told me things that I had never said to her about what had happened in the house. It was strange to me to hear that said back to me. It wasn't very comfortable."

The neighbour had specific instructions for Andrea. "She told me to give her a stone; I had some large stones downstairs. She took it upstairs to the den and put the stone down in a certain place. She warned us, 'Whatever you do just don't move it.' We asked why and she said, 'All the entity's negative energy had been contained in there. If you move it, it will release.'"

Andrea was able to report that since that time, the ghostly disturbances have "died down to a point where it's very unusual to have something happen. Before, it was 10 times a day that something would happen. I don't know what she [the woman who blessed the house] did, but the stone is still there in the corner of that room. I'm not moving it. It's just there permanently. If I move, I'm leaving it; if whoever moves in after me wants to unleash it, then go ahead, it's your place."

Although Andrea has found it easier to cope with the resident spirit since the blessing and since she's matured into young adulthood, she's still looking forward to moving out of the haunted house.

She's also still puzzled by the haunting. "The house was new. Nothing like this ever bothered me before. I liked the house before we moved in. Nobody ever died here."

She summed up the terrible mystery the only way she could, by simply saying, in a low, quiet voice, "I just don't know."

Tainted Townhouse

Positive energy, and lots of it, exuded from Jennifer's voice over the telephone line. "Oh, I tell you, it's really changed our perception of things. We have a new appreciation for the other side," she began.

This was going to be a great interview, I was sure. And I was correct, but in a very different way than I'd anticipated. The following is, almost exclusively in Jennifer's words, a chronicle of the supernatural events that this young woman, her husband, Steve, and their newborn daughter, Britney, endured for the five months they lived in their newly constructed townhouse in northeast Calgary.

Excited about their first real estate purchase, Steve and Jennifer drove out to see the place "before it was finished. It was under construction, only in the framing stage. We walked in to have a look around. All of a sudden there was a spew of water in the basement. Either the water line had burst or [the water] was left on."

After phoning the utility company's emergency service department, there was little the couple could do. "We sat there and waited for them to come and turn the main valve off. I'm not a superstitious person but I said to Steve, 'I wonder if this is an omen.' Steve never forgot that."

The couple was shaken by the experience and they seriously considered buying a different unit in the complex. Despite their concerns, however, Jennifer and Steve moved into the townhouse they had originally chosen.

"We moved in on the May long weekend. We had five budgies at the time. We'd been staying at my in-laws' place and we left the birds there because it was too cold to move them," Jennifer explained.

Once the weather was more agreeable they brought the budgies to the townhouse. The birds' reaction to the new house was immediate. "They went crazy. We couldn't keep them quiet. They were squawking constantly and at all hours of the day. I had to keep their cages covered because they were going absolutely crazy. I thought this was weird, especially as I knew that animals are so perceptive. I wondered why the birds would be fine in one place but not in another."

Searching for a practical explanation for the birds' bizarre behaviour, the young woman reasoned that they might be sensitive to "the smell of the new carpet or the paint." Within a few days, however, Jennifer had little time to be concerned about the pets. Much more important matters were in the family's immediate future.

Steve had previously been a healthy young man, but, "within the first days of moving in, Steve developed a heart arrhythmia. It was so bad that we had to take him to the hospital. There were some changes noted on the heart monitor."

Both Steve and Jennifer were troubled by this turn of events and were deeply puzzled when they noticed something very strange in the house: "If you stood close to the windows at the back of the house you would get that bizarre pressure in your chest like you were going on a roller coaster; a pressure, a flutter. I couldn't stand to be close to those windows. My father-in-law, who has a heart condition, also felt it when he was in the house. It bothered him so much one time that he had to leave."

To complicate the situation further, Jennifer and Steve were expecting their first child later that summer. The pregnancy had been going so well that, until moving into the townhouse, Jennifer had been able to keep to her normal routine. Shortly after the move, however, the mother-to-be went for what she thought would be a routine medical appointment.

Jennifer recalled, "The obstetrician said, 'You have problems. You must quit work and go on complete bedrest until [the baby] is born.'"

Jennifer immediately did exactly what she had been told to do. "I spent most of my bedrest in the family room on the couch, watching television. In June I heard this funny noise. It sounded like someone was shooting a water sprinkler at the siding on the outside of the house. It would come and go like that but it also sounded like a snow shovel being dragged on pavement—that kind of grating sound. I would look outside and couldn't see anything that could be causing the sound and nobody else seemed to hear it."

In retrospect, Jennifer realized that at that point, she was in denial. She had watched a television documentary about hauntings and noted many similarities between what she and Steve were experiencing in this townhouse and the generally accepted signs that a paranormal being was present. That being, Jennifer now suspects, was angered by her denial. The haunting became "progressively worse," as did the medical concerns about her previously trouble-free pregnancy.

The forced physical inactivity allowed Jennifer plenty of time to consider the increasingly strange situation. One reason she chose the family room to rest in was that in the living room it felt like there was "an old man in the corner chair. All he [did was] stare at me. I couldn't even stand to be in that room. I'd look in that corner and not want to make eye contact."

Steve was sympathetic to Jennifer's reactions because there were places in the house that disturbed him as well. "Neither of us could handle going downstairs to do the laundry. We'd be constantly looking over our shoulder toward the furnace where the water had been spewing. The basement was an uncomfortable place."

Jennifer and Steve could no longer deny the mounting signs that they were living in a haunted house. Toward the end of her pregnancy, Jennifer explained that she was allowed a little more flexibility in her routine. "I was vacuuming in a hallway between the kitchen and the living room. It was not a narrow hallway, my piano was there. All of a sudden this air brushed by me quite deliberately. It was cold air. It swooshed by me. I stopped and thought *That felt like a ghost going by me!*"

Near the end of the summer, Jennifer and Steve's baby daughter, Britney, was born. There were complications for both mother and child but, working as a team and with support from both of their sets of parents, they managed day by day.

"When Britney was only a week to 10 days old we had her in the crib. I had been sleeping but we had the nursery monitor on. All of a sudden I heard heavy breathing on the monitor—like a man's breath—very intense—like an obscene phone call."

Hoping against all reality, Jennifer wondered for a

moment if her husband was in with the baby, "but he was lying beside me."

Three days later the new parents went to get their tiny infant up in the morning and found her lying in a completely different position than they had laid her in hours before. "We thought, 'Oh, how precocious. Our little baby can move around the crib. She was our first so we had no clue. We mentioned it to my mother-in-law and my mother. They both said that one of us must have moved her and just didn't tell the other, but the crib was set up so that the blankets were tucked in at one end. We always put her in the same position. We would never have disrupted the bedding. We both knew that neither of us did that."

Jennifer's concerns about her daughter's bedroom were growing. "I never felt comfortable in the back part of the house. One of the back bedrooms happened to be Britney's. The whole time I prepared her nursery I didn't feel comfortable.

"I went to take a shower in the mornings when Steve was home and I'd hear Britney screaming and crying. I'd get out of the shower and say, 'Steve, how could you let her cry like that?' He'd tell me she hadn't been crying at all but I heard a baby crying at the top of her lungs." Understandably, Jennifer was extremely upset by these sounds.

Another time Jennifer tried to have a shower, she "put Britney into her crib, turned on the mobile and hopped into the shower. When I got out she had a receiving blanket over her face. I told Steve and he said that I must have left some blankets around but I didn't and how would she have pulled [a blanket] on to herself? It was perfectly folded, like it had just come off the change table and been placed on her face."

More frightening experiences occurred. "When Britney was about 10 days old, I walked up the stairs. Something pulled me back. It leaned me at a 45-degree angle and then stood me back up again. It had full support of me. It was like someone had me on a board and had just tilted me back and then tipped me forward. I tried to deny [this was happening]. We wanted to turn a blind eye to it but this thing was trying to get us out of there because this was his space."

Everyone's health was now in jeopardy. "Britney got sick—sicker and sicker. She would get these rashes all over her body and all of a sudden become upset. We couldn't calm her down. We didn't know what to do. As soon as I would take her out of the house, get her into the car seat and drive away from the place, she stopped crying. She was perfect at my Mom's place and at my mother-in-law's but as soon as we got home she'd scream."

With all the best intentions, the two grandmothers tried to assure Jennifer that there was nothing seriously wrong. "You must be nervous," one would suggest. "Maybe the baby's too warm" or "you're holding her too much," the other would offer.

"I didn't know what to make of it. Every time I'd take her to the doctor, by the time I got there, the rash would be gone but when I got her back home, there was the rash again. Worse, sometimes her face would change. Her eyes would go dark and evil. Then she would come back to the little baby that I knew. I'd shake my head and think *What did I just see?* It happened to me five or six times. Her face would just change to this evil—'evil eyes' is the only way I can describe it. She didn't even look like my baby. Then she'd turn back as I held her in my arms."

Jennifer continued: "Things got progressively worse. One day I woke up in the morning and opened the drapes. There was a dead pigeon on my lawn. I thought at first that a cat must have got it." The more Jennifer looked at the corpse, the less possible that seemed. The bird had been plucked clean of its feathers, which lay in a neat pile beside the bird's body. Stranger still, "it was windy but the feathers weren't blowing away. Steve got rid of the bird but I wondered, maybe this was a symbol. Everything that was happening seemed very symbolic.

"I remember, too, trying to do some paperwork at the kitchen table. I couldn't concentrate but again, it was toward the back of the house, near the family room. I thought *What the heck is this?* It was like I was on some kind of medication or something. I couldn't do my work in that space. You could almost draw a line, front to back of this house, where you started to feel terrible."

Jennifer began to experience serious health problems during this period and was admitted back into the hospital with post-childbirth complications. Her sister offered to bring Jennifer's toiletries from home to the hospital. The favour was not as easy to accomplish as had been expected. Jennifer explained, "My sister said she felt uneasy. She opened the linen closet and there was a funny smell. She just grabbed whatever personal items I had in there. My mom went over to the townhouse that day too. She brought her dog with her. The poor thing was shaking and whining so badly. It wet on the carpet, which it never does."

The dog was as disturbed as the budgies had been, and every member of the household had now suffered some serious medical problem. In an attempt to normalize the situation somewhat, Jennifer returned, on a part-time basis, to her profession, while her mother-in-law looked after Britney. When Jennifer returned home the first day, she found her mother-in-law very agitated. The young mother was informed in no uncertain terms that she would "have to get a new nursery monitor. This one's terrible."

Apparently the woman had put her granddaughter to bed upstairs in the crib and turned on the monitor. When she got downstairs to the receiving monitor, it was hissing with static. Wondering what it was she was hearing, the woman put the device up against her ear. "All of a sudden there was an explosion of sound in her ear that almost blew her ear off. She shook it a little bit, tried to plug it into different outlets but there was still the static. She turned the volume up and put it to her ear—WHAM!—another explosion of sound, so she brought Britney downstairs and kept her there until I got home. As soon as I did, my mother-in-law couldn't wait to get out of my condo. I've never seen her so flustered. She said, 'I have to go. We're leaving for Vancouver and I have to pack and get ready.'"

At that point, Jennifer paused for just a moment in her recounting. "It was right after that, in the early morning hours of a September day, that we saw it. Steve was up to feed Britney. He was sitting in the family room when he heard the grating noise, like there's water shooting at the house, that I'd been telling him about. He checked the underground sprinklers and they weren't on. He turned off the inside lights, just left the stove hood light on, and went to the back door. That's when he saw this hooded figure walk across the backyard, along the fence, toward the neighbour's. He came and woke me up. He said, 'Come downstairs. You have to see this.' "

Jennifer followed her husband to the back door of the townhouse. "The figure came from the backyard toward the family room window. It came right to us. It was levitated, probably 6 feet off the ground already because we had stairs going down to the backyard from the kitchen door. It was hooded. It had no face. It was a three-quarter-length figure. You couldn't see its feet. It moved. It floated up toward the bedrooms. It was like the Grim Reaper."

Nearly panicked, the pair ran upstairs. They had left Britney asleep on their bed. They knew then that they would have to leave. Steve's parents were visiting Vancouver, so their house was available as a temporary respite. They also knew they would have to explain their seemingly impulsive actions.

"Everyone we told this to said, 'Oh, you saw fog,' but fog does not have a shape like this did. It does not move like this did. It does not maintain a form and do what Steve and I saw it do."

Not surprisingly, Jennifer was unable to get back to sleep that night. "I called my mother at five o'clock in the morning. She said, 'You've got to get out of there.' At six o'clock I saw our friend and neighbour, Jim, pull up to his condo."

Jennifer called out an invitation to the man to come in for a minute. As she was telling him what had occurred, she "heard this guttural, wordless, creepy grunt in my right ear. I turned and looked in that direction and it stopped. I turned away and it started again. I told Steve and he said, 'That's it, we're out of here.' We just took what we were wearing and a couple of things for Britney and we left."

Although the family had physically escaped the tainted townhouse, they were still heavily involved financially. This situation had to be corrected. "We called a psychology professor. We called the church and met with Father Black [a pseudonym], who works with the paranormal. He came over to the house, walked right over to the family room window and said, 'Something's not right here.'"

Jennifer was amazed at his accuracy. He had picked out the exact spot where, just five days before they'd seen the apparition, Britney had suffered a frightening and medically puzzling seizure.

The priest then enlisted the aid of a prayer group. Jennifer and Steve could not understand the group's Latin pleas, but they and Britney had violent physical reactions to the prayer session.

Having done what they could, they "put the place up for sale." Although the rest of the development had not sold out by that time, they held out hope. "We said a prayer. We said, 'God, you have to get us out of here.'"

Despite their own desperation, Steve and Jennifer had agreed between themselves that they wouldn't sell the place to anyone with children. Moments later a bachelor approached the couple and a deal was soon struck. They were finally free of the building that had taken them "literally to hell and back." The healing process could, and did, begin.

Jennifer and Steve have settled happily into a new house. They have welcomed a second daughter and generally rebuilt their lives from the detritus left after five months in an evilly haunted house.

When reflecting upon our lengthy conversation, I found myself wondering if people with less strength, resources and vitality could have won the battle against such an evil and determined spirit. Hopefully, we'll never have to find out.

Chapter 2

Animals

The bond between people and animals can span time,

place and even death.

Guide Dog

Mary Pennington of Veteran, Alberta, has had many experiences that can't be explained by ordinary means. She's quite philosophical about these occurrences by now, stating only that "nature and the world around us often talks to us, if only we listen and believe."

One of the most dramatic and convincing encounters occurred when a mystical dog escorted seven-year-old Mary safely home. Mary began her story by explaining that neighbourly lending and borrowing "was common in those days."

"My mother asked me to go to the neighbour's to borrow some tea. The cattle trail I needed to follow was about three-quarters of a mile [1.2 kilometres] across a treed section. In daylight it was fun to follow, with birds' nests to look at and little animals to see. I hurried there as I knew I'd get milk and cookies from the nice neighbour lady."

Mary continued, "Starting home was fine; I played along the way without noticing the dust and rain clouds gathering overhead until the surroundings had become pitch black."

The sudden change in her familiar surroundings frightened and disoriented the little girl. She began "running, trying to find the right path. I was frantic. It was impossible, I was completely lost. The thunder seemed just above my head. The lightning flashes only showed scary glimpses of where I was. It was all so frighteningly different. The rain came in force. I was desperately lost."

Just as panic was flooding through the little girl's mind and body, threatening to paralyze her, "I felt a safe presence beside me. Reaching my hand out, I felt the soft fur of a big dog beside me. Being a country child, I loved animals and felt no fear, just a safe, relaxing feeling."

Trusting this strange animal that had suddenly and mysteriously come to her side, Mary said, "I stuffed the tea container in my dress to keep it dry and the dog led me along the right winding path for home. I felt calm and sure. As we came out of the thicker bush I was glad to see the lamplight from our house. A few more steps and there was my mother carrying the lantern. She was coming to look for me. We ran into each other's arms. I could still feel the dog's presence."

Confident that her mother would let her keep the dog that had saved her life, Mary looked down at her side where the dog had been. "There was no dog there. I called and called. We both tried to hunt for him amongst the trees and the wet grass. He was so friendly and helpful that he'd never have run away."

Maybe not but, undeniably, the rescue animal had disappeared as mysteriously as it had appeared when Mary needed assistance so badly. "No dog of that description was ever seen."

To this day the enigma has never been solved. Not surprisingly, though, Mary never forgot the encounter. To some degree it prepared her to be more accepting of the mysteries that surround us through life.

Sadie's Goodbye

Norma Kuerbis lives in the town of Rochester, some 30 kilometres south of Athabasca. Norma is sure that the spirit of her much loved dog, Sadie, stayed behind until Norma's adult daughter, Ramona, had a chance to get back to the family home and say goodbye to the deceased dog. The young woman and the dog had been very close. "Sadie used to sleep in the bedroom that Ramona used," Norma explained.

Sadie enjoyed a long and happy life, producing four litters of puppies during her life of 14 years. She was a companion to the family as well as to Thumber and Duke, the two other dogs in the household. By early 1982, however, Sadie's health began to fail. "She began to have heart

Sadie's spirit waited in Ramona's bedroom until the young woman could get back to say goodbye.

problems. In March when Sadie got too bad, we had to take her into the vet's. She never came home."

Norma immediately noticed a changed in her other pets' behaviour. They would no longer go into Ramona's bedroom. "They would stop, look where Sadie used to stay, then walk away. This happened every time the dogs tried to enter." Norma began to think that Sadie's spirit was keeping the other dogs out of the room by haunting it because she was waiting there to say goodbye to Ramona. "After about two months Ramona came home for a visit. Thumber and Duke were delighted to see her. I noticed after she walked into the bedroom the dogs went in too. They were no longer afraid. I believe that Sadie was waiting to say goodbye. She was able to do this when Ramona came home. After that, all was fine."

Longhaired Apparition

In 1991, Debbie and Jim were living in a cooperative housing development in St. Albert and happily awaiting the birth of their first child. They had two five-year-old tabby cats, Mouse and Leo. Although the two animals were brother and sister, they were as different as their names implied. Mouse was tiny, easily frightened and shorthaired, while Leo was longhaired and loved to interact with people. Unlike most cats, this one was overtly affectionate and had even learned to do some tricks.

After the couple set up the crib in the nursery, Leo jumped right into it, made himself completely at home and even stretched out for a catnap. No matter how many times, or how forcefully, Debbie removed the cat from "his" comfortable new bed, if the door to that room was open, Leo would get into the crib.

With the impending birth, Leo's habit of jumping in the crib became a real concern. They couldn't keep the nursery door closed while the newborn slept, yet if they didn't, they feared that Leo would inadvertently harm the baby. The situation seemed almost unsolvable as the cats were important members of the household. Debbie had adopted them when they were just a few weeks old and had nursed Leo through some serious illnesses.

As it would turn out, the hand of fate reached out and solved the developing problem permanently. Leo's health once again began to fail and it became clear that he was suffering terribly. Debbie and Jim took him to a veterinarian, and the news was not good. The couple brought the cat home, aware that they had a difficult decision to make. After much thought and consideration, they left Leo asleep in the house while they went back to the vet's office to make the appointment to have the cat put out of his misery. By the time they got home, Leo had died, peacefully, in his sleep.

No longer would anyone ever have to worry about the trick-playing, comfort-loving cat hurting the baby who was soon to make his entrance into the world. Both Debbie and Jim knew that they would miss the cat terribly and were very upset that they hadn't been able to say goodbye to their unique pet. Little did Debbie know that Leo would soon rectify the lack of closure she was feeling.

Being pregnant, Debbie was not sleeping well and was making frequent trips to the bathroom through the night. It was during one of these sojourns that Debbie saw Leo's image waiting for her in the hall. "He was so real that I bent down to pat him," she explained. Then, just as suddenly as he had appeared, the animal's manifestation vanished.

Leo, a cat like no other, had come back—if only for a quick goodbye.

Continuing Presences

In each of the next two stories the pet owners saw that their beloved animals were dying and, rather than see them suffer through to the bitter end, had them put to sleep. From what happened after those instances of euthanasia, I've come to wonder if the animals' spirits initially failed to realize that their physical selves no longer existed on this plane.

Brewster was an exceptionally large bassett hound with extraordinarily long, floppy ears. Whenever he woke up from one of his many naps through the day, Brewster would shake his head vigorously and his ears would flap noisily against his head—a very distinctive sound.

When the dog became ill with a lung disease, Brewster's owners braced themselves for the dog's final trip to the vet's office. Oddly, for several days after the dog had been "put to sleep," the owners would occasionally hear the familiar sound of their dog's long ears flapping as if he were still there and shaking his head when he awoke from a nap.

"This only happened for a few days," they explained to me. "Then the sound stopped. It was as if it took that long for Brewster to realize that he was dead. We don't know for sure, but perhaps he didn't completely leave us until the time he was going to have died from the disease."

PJ was a petite tabby cat that, judging by a couple of random orange spots on her fur, must have had at least one calico ancestor. She also had attitude, lots of it, and was often seen chasing much larger cats off "her" property. By the time this once-active cat was 17 years of age, however, she had slowed down and become a virtual house cat. She was losing weight at an alarming rate and sleeping nearly 24 hours

The ghost of PJ the cat could be heard trotting down the stairs to join her people—for several days after her death.

a day. When her owners noticed that she was limping during her odd periods of activity, the couple decided the formerly spunky cat should not suffer any longer.

Not surprisingly, the trip home from the vet's office was quiet for the owners, as was the evening that followed—until they heard the distinct, but impossible, sound of PJ trotting down the basement stairs to join them watching television. Although no image was ever visible, for the balance of that week, the spirit of the elderly cat kept to the routine she had developed in life and was heard making her way down the stairs to join "her people."

Like Brewster the bassett hound, it simply took a little while for PJ the cat to become aware that she no longer existed in corporeal form.

Special Aid

Deborah Tetley, a reporter with the *Calgary Herald*, called me about a story she was working on for the newspaper. This surprised me only until I learned that it was a ghost story she was tracking down. When the article ran on Valentine's Day and proved to be something of a love story, I was delighted.

It seems some of the staff members at the Calgary Society for Prevention of Cruelty to Animals (SPCA) suspect that Ellen Foster, one of the founders of that branch of the society, has not yet left the shelter on 36 Avenue N.E. that she, effectively, helped to build.

Although Cheryl Wallach, the manager of community relations for the SPCA, would like to remain somewhat skeptical, she did explain to Tetley that there often seems to be a benign presence overlooking the animals and the operation of the society itself. Electric lights that were turned off will be found on. Those that have been left on will be found to have been turned off. Doors open and close when there's no one near them, and once, the cremation room was found empty but locked from the inside.

It's the "quiet patter of the petite woman's footsteps," though, that has the staff convinced the ghost is the spirit of Ellen Foster, who died in 1975. Although the entity seems harmless, she has startled employees such as Stephan Mazubert and sent them running from the building.

Another employee, Tammy Dekens, sensed a presence that she wasn't able to see. She's sure that Ellen Foster's ghost actually brushed past her once. On another occasion Tammy brought her own dog into the shelter with her while she did a little extra work. No matter how Tammy tried to calm her pet, the dog seemed completely, and uncharacteristically, unable to relax. It wasn't until she heard a disembodied voice utter the words "Oh, it's you" that Tammy realized why her dog was so jittery. There were no other human beings in the building, but the ghost was most certainly visiting.

There is little doubt in my mind that the woman who was so lovingly devoted to the care of needy animals in life has continued to watch over them long after her own death.

White Kitty

As a consequence of all the ghost stories I have investigated, I believe that some people are more likely than others to have a paranormal encounter. The following story is just one of the several ghost-related events a particular couple told me about. I found this one especially interesting, though, because it seems to indicate that just as human ghosts are more attracted to receptive folks, animal ghosts gravitate to animal lovers.

Karen and Mike were living in a duplex in Sexsmith, Alberta, when they "adopted a pure white cat from the SPCA."

They named the kitten Slinky, and soon "Slinky became part of our household."

Karen was not surprised, then, when she thought she would hear the cat following her around the house or would see her "whip into a room." What did surprise Karen was when she discovered how frequently she'd been mistaken. Many times when Karen was sure she'd heard or seen Slinky, the cat was nowhere near her. At first, Karen brushed these oddities from her mind. However, that comfortable response was about to be altered.

"In October 1998, a pure white stray cat came to our door and we helped her out by fixing up a doghouse in the backyard and by feeding her regularly. About a month and a half later, *another* pure white female kitten ended up at our doorstep. It was very cold out and Kitsa [as they'd named the second cat] refused to have a housemate, so the kitten [to be named Angel] came in the house to join Slinky."

While Kitsa lived in the doghouse in the yard, Slinky was an integral part of Mike and Karen's household, even sleeping in their bed. "Now, the new addition, Angel, was also included in our nightly settling in for bed."

"The second night we had both cats in our room, I was just finished in the bathroom and [was] turning out the lights in the duplex. There was just enough light to move by and I am very nearsighted, so things were quite blurry without my contact lenses in. As I opened the bedroom door, I saw the shape of a cat whisk out of the room. I tried to catch it and missed. Inside the room, I couldn't tell in the dark which cat had got out, so I turned on the light. Slinky was in the closet and Angel was on the bed. I told my husband, but he did not wish to believe me."

It was Mike's turn next, however. "Sometime later, he was working on his computer when a white cat jumped onto the desk, ran across his keyboard and down to the floor. Slinky was not in the room, Angel had gone to a new home and Kitsa was still outside."

Mike and Karen now realized they were sharing their home with a phantom cat. They began to refer to the presence as "White Kitty." The sightings continued: "I caught sight of it running into my husband's clothing cabinet one evening. It seemed harmless enough, and the cats never acted like they saw anything."

Karen concluded her letter by writing, "We have moved yet one more time. In the last weeks before we moved again, White Kitty didn't show up very often. My husband would see it flitting about, but nothing very dramatic happened until just shortly before we left. I was getting ready for work one morning and my husband was still in bed. I was standing in the kitchen with my back to the table, facing the sink and window. I looked right up the hallway to the bedrooms and saw Kitsa at the end of the hall walking towards me. I turned my head back to the kitchen sink and saw Kitsa out of the corner of my eye running from behind me into the living room, on my left. Then I heard a meow from the hallway and turned back to see Kitsa standing at the edge of the kitchen."

At least some of those sightings were not of Kitsa. They were of the phantom cat, but Karen and Mike still do not know for sure which felines were real and which were merely apparitions.

Another time, Karen said, she was bent over taking off her shoes "when Slinky slipped past me, literally under my nose, and went down into the basement. Two seconds later Slinky went past me down into the basement. Each time this "double cat" thing happened, only one of our live kitties was in evidence."

Karen and Mike eventually became very accepting of their menagerie, live and otherwise. They moved recently and invited White Kitty to come with them. Evidence seems to indicate that their offer was accepted!

Phantom Pet to the Rescue

The following ghost story is one of the most heart-warming supernatural tales I have ever come across. The strange events took place during the summer of 1958 in Wood Buffalo National Park, in the extreme north of Alberta.

In the second week of June that year, the LaCroix family's beloved collie dog, Ruffles, had died. All five members of the household were devastated by the loss, but the three children—13-year-old Denise, 11-year-old Lucille and 6-year-old Jerome—were especially hurt.

Some five weeks after the death of the pet, Mr. and Mrs. LaCroix decided to try to distract the children from their mourning by taking them on an adventure of wilderness camping. After arriving at the campsite, both little girls and their brother were instantly and completely enthralled with their unfamiliar surroundings. They loved exploring the rugged wilderness, so much so that in the early hours of July 22, hours before their parents woke up, Denise, Lucille and Jerome foolishly headed out on a hike by themselves.

Although they didn't intend to travel very far, the children soon realized that they'd become disoriented in the bush and were unable to find the route back to the safety of their parents. Despite their best attempts to quell the rising panic they were all feeling, the trio knew that what they had planned as a little hike had the potential to turn into a life-threatening escapade, especially if they continued to walk around. Using the survival skills their parents had taught them, the children sought shelter under some scrub brush.

When Mr. and Mrs. LaCroix awoke, they immediately began searching the area for their children, but when they didn't find them, they knew that they would need help. Mrs. LaCroix stayed at the camp while Mr. LaCroix drove to the nearest settlement to round up as many volunteer searchers as he possibly could. LaCroix drove the assembled group back to the campsite and had them fan out from there. Mrs. LaCroix continued to stand watch by the tent in the hope that the children would somehow make their way back.

As morning turned to afternoon, the children were huddled together under the scrub, crying piteously and paralyzed by fear. Their parents, of course, were frantic with worry, and the searchers, now spread out in a wide pattern, were quickly becoming discouraged. Suddenly one volunteer, a man named Bob, thought he saw something moving in the bush. At first, he was sure his eyes were playing tricks on him because it looked to be a dog— a collie—with a collar and a tag around its neck.

The dog approached him and allowed itself to be patted. Reaching around the collar to the tag that hung from it, the man read a single engraved word: "Ruffles." The searcher reasoned that was the dog's name. The animal was still for only a moment, though. Soon, it walked away from Bob before stopping and looking back at the stationary man. When the human did not follow, Ruffles approached him again, this time for only a second before walking away and then stopping again. It seemed that the dog wanted the man to follow, so Bob started to walk toward it, also calling to the other searchers to join him. Soon the entire party was following the animal.

Seconds later, though, the dog disappeared. They couldn't find him anywhere. Despite their constant and loud calls of "Ruffles, come here," the animal did not respond.

Not far away, the three LaCroix children were snuggled together on the ground, still whimpering in fear. Then, slowly, each of them in turn thought they could hear men's voices calling out the name of their deceased dog, Ruffles. At first, they couldn't believe their ears. For a moment, Denise actually thought that all of them had already died and were now in heaven with Ruffles. Little Jerome, however, apparently thought differently. He quickly became convinced that his beloved dog had come to find them and he called out to the animal. Of course, the dog could no longer respond, but the searchers who'd been following the phantom animal heard the little boy's cries and found the three lost children. Within the hour, the entire LaCroix family was reunited.

Even in death, the loyal dog served and protected his family.

Unpopular Cat

Ettie Miller lived in Grimshaw, Alberta. Everyone knew that Ettie did not like cats generally and that she disliked her daughter Kathleen's cat especially. The best Ettie could bring herself to do was ignore the cat. Normally, this was reasonably easy as the cat rarely sought Ettie out.

However, on Friday, July 29, 1942, the cat began to make overtures toward Ettie. It would rub up against her legs when she stood and would jump up on her as soon as she sat down. The animal seemed determined to be as close to Ettie as possible, even rubbing up against her face when it had the chance.

Something about the cat had certainly changed, but nothing had changed for Ettie. She still disliked the creature and would put it down and shoo it away whenever it came near. Despite being rebuffed, the cat continued to be affectionate toward Ettie and in a last-ditch attempt to get some peace, the woman locked the cat into the next room.

Although no one could figure out any reason for the cat's bizarre behaviour at the time, they were soon able to connect it to a tragedy many, many miles away. Ettie's son, a member of Canada's Armed Forces, had been killed in action at exactly the time his sister's cat had changed its behaviour so radically.

The cat continued to fuss over Ettie for the next two weeks before, slowly, its interest in the woman simply dissipated as mysteriously as it had begun. Perhaps the spirit of Ettie's son had become adjusted to the fact that he was no longer part of our earthly plane. Not surprisingly,

Ettie's attitude toward the animal changed considerably once she suspected that it was connected somehow to her deceased son's spirit. Even after the cat began to return to its previous aloof attitude, Ettie was always sure to have some kind of a treat ready when she knew she was going to see the animal.

Chapter 3

Relatives Return

Tales of deceased relatives returning to visit the living

are a staple of ghost lore.

Offering Assurance?

I have known the woman who recounted the following experiences on a casual basis for several years. She holds a position at a local service business in Edmonton, and any interactions she and I ever had were in connection with her career, not mine. For this reason I was very surprised when she indicated that she would like to talk to me. Because of the highly personal nature of this supernatural encounter and the woman's standing in the community, my informant has asked that I not reveal her identity but refer to her as Emily.

She began by explaining that, although the encounters went on for several days, the whole paranormal experience began very suddenly.

"I woke up at about 4:20 in the morning on the Thursday before Christmas of 1999. It was the heat that woke me up. I just couldn't stand it. It was just so terribly hot in the house. I went upstairs and checked the thermostat. The thermostat was fine, it wasn't [set too high] but still I could feel this terrible heat, almost a suffocating heat."

Not knowing what else to do, Emily headed back downstairs. "There are seven steps from the upper level to the main entrance and then seven more steps to go down [to the lower level]. When I got to the landing [between the sets of steps] I saw this really beautiful white, such a piercing white that you couldn't see through it. It was a tall figure walking from one bedroom toward our bedroom. Then it was gone."

Emily stood staring in amazement and thinking about what she'd just seen. "It was a tall slender figure. It was beautiful white, brighter than snow. It didn't hurt the eyes or anything. I just stood there for a moment and I wondered *Did I see right?* Then I proceeded to go down the stairs in the dark. I didn't see anything but when I got down to the end of the stairs I switched the light on. I still couldn't see anything. At that point I got terrified because I know what I saw but where did it go?"

Being a practical woman, Emily "switched off the light and ran into bed. I woke my husband up and I told him that I'd seen something, that I thought I'd seen a ghost. He said, 'Yeah, yeah, whatever.' It was 5:15 [by then] and our [radio] alarm clock went off although it wasn't set to go off until 6:45."

Even this Emily knew was not normal, for the radio was between stations and the volume was turned up "full blast." Worse, the audio that it *was* transmitting was heavily mixed with static.

"We tried to switch the radio off and we couldn't. We tried switching the stations and we couldn't do that either. It just kept playing and playing. Finally the music stopped. We went back to bed but five minutes later the same thing happened, the loud music came on and we couldn't get it to switch off. Again we couldn't change the station. Even if we changed the station, the radio was still broadcasting the same music. No matter which button we tried to switch, it would not shut off. It played for a few more moments and then it finally switched off on its own. Then it did it again five minutes after that. In total this happened three times in fifteen minutes."

What was stranger still was that Emily and her husband *always* set the clock radio to the "alarm" setting, "never" to the radio setting because with "music we just will fall back to sleep."

Emily's husband was suspicious that an electrical problem had caused the strange occurrence. In order to rule this possibility out, "the next morning," Emily explained, "I asked the lady who lives behind us in the fourplex if she'd had any electrical problems or anything like that. She said, 'No, no, everything's fine,' so I didn't say anything else to her.

"The next day I got home from work and went downstairs. I was going to work out on the treadmill. My son was leaving the house to go to the gym so we said our goodbyes and I got on the treadmill," Emily told me. Emily wore a personal stereo with headphones while working out in order to have some music to jog along to.

Despite having the headphones on and hearing music playing directly into her ears, Emily "could feel thumping or stomping of feet but it wasn't coming from upstairs on the floor. It was just from mid-air. I thought *Okay, something's really odd* because I play my music quite loudly and normally I don't hear anything else. I knew I was alone in the house and so I turned the treadmill down some to a lower speed and shut the portable stereo off. Then I didn't hear the thumping anymore, but I had a strange sensation that somebody was in the room with me. I thought, *Okay, enough of this treadmill thing.* I was going to go for a shower. The television was on with the volume quite low. I went downstairs and thought, *No, I'm not going to have a shower because then I have to pull the curtain closed.*"

Emily decided that taking a bath would be easier on her jarred nerves. "I just got into the tub and the TV started blaring really, really loudly. I thought, *Oh, no, this*

can't be happening ... I grabbed my robe and I was going
up the stairs. As I got to the landing, the sound on the television went down to its regular volume again. I checked
the remote control and discovered it was set to the right
volume."

Abandoning the idea of a bath, Emily simply spent the
balance of her evening trying to relax. "We went to bed and
toward morning, the alarm clock went off again three times
for the same number of minutes [each time]. By then my
husband was also thinking something [paranormal] is happening here, especially after I told him about what had
happened the previous evening."

Emily acknowledged, "I was getting a little scared. I
went to work the next day. After I came home that afternoon, I was by myself, doing laundry. I was folding towels in
our utility room. In that room there's just the one door. My
washer and dryer are on one wall and on the other's my
deep freezer. I was taking the towels out of the dryer and my
back was toward the door."

The haunting she'd been enduring was about to take a
much more frightening turn. "I could feel this hot presence
again. It was really electrifying. It was just so terribly hot. I
turned around and there was nobody there but it was hot
just by the doorway. It wasn't hot in the rest of the room.
Whatever this was, it just kind of lingered in that one area at
the doorway. I folded up my towels and said to myself, out
loud, 'I'm going to take these towels into the linen closet.' I
did that and then I went upstairs but I could feel the presence of this heat again, in the kitchen this time.

"The area of heat stayed with me for about an hour
and a half. I was doing baking, taking my time, cleaning

everything up and then I said out loud to myself, 'I think I'm going to set up the Christmas tree.'"

Those words were no sooner out of Emily's mouth than she "could feel the presence coming down the hallway. It stopped at the living room. I brought out my Christmas ornaments. It didn't do anything [and then] it just was gone. In the meantime, I noticed that this presence, the heat, was only felt in the kitchen, in the hall downstairs but it never went into any actual rooms. Whatever it was respected our privacy I think."

Perhaps having had quite enough of being alone under such unusual circumstances, Emily phoned one of her sisters. After hearing about the strange goings-on in Emily's home, the sister reminded her of an event some months earlier. The two had been chatting on the phone then too. They were talking about their nephew who had just passed away and how hard their other sister, the lad's mother, was taking the unexpected death. Emily explained to me that during that call, she had been sitting on a rocking chair in the living room, at the patio doors.

"Suddenly, I said to my sister, 'This is strange. Someone's just walked past our living room window.' That's impossible because it's almost 8 to 10 feet [2 to 3 metres] off the ground. It was a clear white shadow. It couldn't have been a reflection from the streetlights or cars because we would've seen them before."

At the time, Emily put the bizarre incident out of her mind. It wasn't until this conversation with her sister that she remembered the image and began to connect *that* sighting with what had been happening in her home recently.

Emily continued, "My sister said, 'Well, that almost sounds like what you saw go by your window.' When I thought back, yes, it was very white but not quite as bright as what I saw in my house, but the difference might just have been simply the difference between inside light and outside light."

"I always referred to this presence as a 'he,' why I don't know. My nephew was tall and slender [like the image]."

As Emily concluded the recounting of the strange events, she did mention that another reason she thinks that the presence she saw and sensed might have been the spirit of her nephew was that when she had some time to herself, she "would kind of say a little prayer. I'd say 'Let us know that you're all right,' so I don't know if this might be because of that."

Emily cannot know for sure what it was that she saw, sensed and felt or why it came to her. All she can say for sure is, "I know that what I saw was real."

The Watchers

Wilma takes justifiable pride in her beautiful home and garden. It seems to have been enhanced in almost every way. She is sure that the spirit of her mother, among others, has visited her there. This photo taken by her daughter, Linda, when no one was in or near the house, seems to show two female figures at the windows beside the garage. Wilma and Linda feel that they are the ghostly images of Wilma's mother and grandmother, both of whom were also skilled and devoted gardeners.

Wilma's long-deceased mother and grandmother appear to look out from the windows at the side of the garage.

Sir Oliver Lodge's Visit

I'm often asked if interest in ghost stories is a new phenomenon. Research tells me that tales of the supernatural have always intrigued us. As recently as this year a ghost story made the headlines of the *Calgary Herald*, but ghost stories have regularly been recounted in Alberta newspapers over the years, ever since we've had newspapers in Alberta.

On April 27, 1920, for instance, the now-defunct newspaper *The Albertan* ran a two-column report about the psychic experiences of a prestigious visitor from England. Sir Oliver Lodge was a physicist whose work was instrumental in the eventual development of the radio. Lodge, accompanied by his wife (referred to only as Lady Lodge) was touring Canada giving lectures at various centres. Sadly, the Lodges' son had died not long before the time of his parents' visit to Canada. Judging by the bereaved parents' activity while they were staying in Alberta, the two were clearly proponents of spiritualism.

Arthur Deighton, an Edmonton art dealer as well as, apparently, a medium, travelled to the Palliser Hotel in Calgary where the Lodges were staying. While there, Deighton also talked to a reporter from *The Albertan*. He spoke of a meeting with the Lodges that by today's terms could best be described as a séance.

To quote the 80-year-old article, "According to Deighton, he gained access to the spirit world through the medium of a special Ouija board which he had made ... and ... that he gave both Sir Oliver Lodge and Lady Lodge a message from their son."

He "went to his suite at the Palliser and settled down at the Ouija board. He said he got into communication with his great-grandfather, Major Frederick Deighton, who served in the Foot Guards at London, England, during the reign of King William IV. Through his great-grandfather, he said he got into communication with Raymond Lodge, who asked him to give his mother, Lady Lodge, a message of hope, as he feared she was slowly dying of grief.

"Deighton then said that he obtained an introduction to Lady Lodge, advised her of the message and was invited to visit the Lodges' suite in the Palliser, where he relayed the son's message to the mother. In the middle of the message, Sir Oliver entered the room. As he was about to withdraw again, Mr. Deighton said that Raymond Lodge called out to his father to stay. At the conclusion of Raymond Lodge's message to his parents he advised them that he would watch over them and prepare everything for them 'when you come home.'

"Mr. Deighton said that Sir Oliver and Lady Lodge were greatly impressed by the event and he quoted the distinguished couple as saying that 'it was the most remarkable instance of our Canadian tour.'"

As a kicker, and perhaps to enhance the credibility of his article, the long-ago scribe added a final sentence: "Mr. Deighton also claims that he received messages for Tyrone Power and his company from Sir Henry Irving."

Considering that article ran more than 80 years ago, not much has changed. Stories of the paranormal still make the news.

Grandma's Goodbye

The following story is a great example of "psychic knowing." This incident goes a long way toward supporting the theory that our minds, or our hearts, or our souls are, in some way we don't fully understand, strongly connected to those we love.

Dawn Rene's letter was so explicit that to paraphrase it would be to risk losing some of its impact. For this reason, I present this young woman's experiences in her own words.

Coming up on five years ago, my paternal grandmother, who lived in Great Falls, Montana, suffered for a few days from what was thought to be stomach flu. My aunt (my grandma's daughter) became concerned when the stomach bug didn't seem to clear up in a day or two and, as my grandma was also diabetic and on dialysis, my aunt decided to check my grandma into one of the hospitals in Great Falls, as a precaution.

My aunt contacted my mom and dad to tell them the news and told them not to worry because all they were going to do in the hospital was run some tests. The thought was that the "stomach bug" may be a gall bladder problem but, again, no one was particularly concerned that it was anything critical.

I heard this news through a phone call and

I was reassured that her hospitalization was a precaution only and not to worry. With that in mind, I went on about my household chores, vacuuming and dusting my basement in our house here in Edmonton. I listened to music and kept working from early afternoon onward.

Suddenly, without any prior feelings of sadness or "blues," I sat down on the couch and cried, I mean sobbed hard, almost hysterically, for roughly 15 or 20 minutes.

After [that time], I dried my eyes, not really understanding what had just happened to me. I went on with my housework until the phone rang at approximately 4:30 PM. It was my father on the phone telling me that my grandmother had passed away that afternoon. I was in a state of shock then and didn't think to ask about what time she had died.

It was not until a couple of days later, after my husband and I had travelled to Great Falls, Montana, for my grandmother's funeral that I remembered to ask someone at what time my grandmother had died. My uncle said they weren't exactly sure, but that the doctors had pegged it at sometime between 3 and 3:10 PM.

I was amazed at this because my crying spell had started just after 3 PM that day and had lasted until 3:15 or 3:20. On some deep inner level, I knew my grandmother was dead before I'd actually been told. This doesn't surprise me because she and I were very close in life.

Somehow, the love between Dawn and her grandmother connected the two during the older woman's death, in that very real way that we do not yet fully understood.

Grandma's Wish Granted

One of the questions I'm asked most frequently is "Where do you get your ghost stories?" The answers to that question are as varied as the tales I collect. A woman who was a student in a writing-related course that I taught told me the following incident. Christina was kind enough to get back in touch with me after the sessions were over when she realized that a series of events that had happened to her and her family would be interesting to me.

These events took place immediately after the death of Christina's grandmother while the young woman was trying to, in her words, "appease the last wishes of my grandmother."

The story actually began before the older woman's death when she insisted to Christina's mother that "she be buried in a Ukrainian outfit that she had lovingly sewn for herself." The elderly woman also specified that no one was to sell the special outfit "for a healthy profit."

As it turned out, when the older woman died in 1988, the outfit could neither be used as burial clothes nor could it be sold because, as Christina stated, "when my grandmother died, the Ukrainian outfit mysteriously disappeared."

Christina continued, "My mother could not find it and was forced to bury her mother in regular clothes. Shortly afterward, my mother found the outfit. Not wanting to keep it on her hands, she sold it in a garage sale!"

The dead woman's daughter's solution to the dilemma clearly did not please her mother's spirit. From that point on, Christina recalled, "It seemed that ... our family was somewhat cursed with continuous bad luck and," she added in a dramatically understated fashion, "the house my grandmother [had] lived in, was haunted."

How did they know this? Christina explained: "Because of a fight he had with my father, my brother, who was 16 at the time, moved out of my parents' house on the night of the funeral. That night he experienced a frightful haunting."

Although no details of this frightful haunting were provided, Christina continued on to note that her family dealt with the haunted house the same way they had dealt with the Ukrainian clothing that was found too late—they sold it.

"The house was sold several times [but] was owned by each owner for only a brief period of time," according to Christina.

This supernatural phenomenon bothered most members of the deceased woman's family and it was a frequent topic of discussion. One of those discussions took place in 1995 between Christina and her aunt. They "came up with a way to try to at least symbolically satisfy my grandmother's last wishes. We were going to make our own

Ukrainian outfit and place it on her grave. I dug up a black velvet vest, there was also a skirt, everything was oddly sized and no match for the beautiful outfit my grandmother had made, but we hoped that the thought would count."

Christina continued, "I put the outfit in a bag along with a signed card to my grandmother. I went out to the cemetery on a cold January day, trudged through very deep snow and placed the gift on my grandmother's grave."

Now, all the family could do was wait to see if Christina's kind gesture appeased her grandmother's restless and angry spirit. Over time, it was apparently proven that the gesture had been effective.

"After that, our luck changed back to more or less normal and the house remained owned by someone for an extended period of time."

I last communicated with Christina just last year and she was happy to report that her family's lives no longer feel affected by the ghost of her grandmother whose soul, presumably, is enjoying a peaceful eternity.

A Light-veiled Form

Robert Staysko's experience with a phantom in his house is recounted in Chapter 1 (p. 44). Nearly 15 years after that incident, Robert's father, Andrew Joseph Staysko, died in a hospital bed in Lethbridge, Alberta. Robert and Robert's son Stephen were with Andrew as his spirit left his body.

After the death, the father and son stayed the night with relatives in a nearby family home so that everyone would be together the next day to begin to make the necessary arrangements for the funeral and burial.

Robert explained that "on the night of my father's death (July 29, 1983) the weather was very hot, and the home, being devoid of air conditioning … was very uncomfortable. I was given the main bedroom, my aunt was to sleep in the other bedroom and Stephen was assigned to a cot on the front porch."

During that evening Robert's father's body was "delivered to a funeral home in north Lethbridge which was located about six blocks north of the old family home [where they were staying] … the home that was my father's pride and joy."

The Stayskos turned in early. Slowly, Robert drifted off to sleep. The home where Robert and Stephen were staying was also, temporarily, home to another family member's dog. Through the night Robert heard what he thought to be the dog's restless pacing about the house. "I recall waking a number of times as the dog walked into my bedroom and out again. I slept on my right side with my back to the door and the hallway. I could hear the dog's claws as [the dog] walked off the carpet in the living room onto the linoleum in the hallway and my bedroom. I recall being [disturbed] about every half hour when the dog walked into my bedroom, stood for a moment and then walked out." Robert didn't bother turning over to check why the dog was walking around, as he assumed the dog was just uncomfortable because of the heat and therefore unable to sleep.

Some hours later, toward morning, "as the sky started to lighten, the dog walked in again. I awoke [and] decided to turn over to try to determine why the dog was so restless. As I turned on my left side and looked into the hallway, I saw a light-veiled form standing in the middle of the hallway. As I tried to focus my eyes on it, it moved toward the exit to the living room. Each time I moved my eyes to obtain a clearer view, the apparition moved a little closer to the living room exit."

Robert got out of bed in an attempt to discern exactly what the manifestation was. A moment later, it was evident that Robert's aunt too, had also seen the bizarre form. Whatever the disturbance was, it had certainly not been caused by the dog wandering throughout the house, for Robert "found the dog fast asleep on the kitchen floor."

Next he checked on his son. "I walked to the front porch and found Stephen fast asleep on the cot."

What, then, was this elusive entity that had been so active throughout the night? "It struck me later that the body of my father, who had passed away 12 hours earlier, was lying in a funeral home a few blocks north of the bedroom I was sleeping in at the time. After my father's funeral, I had an opportunity to describe the incident to Father J. Sullivan. He listened with interest and then advised that he was aware of such things happening. It was called a paranormal experience, a supernatural experience, [one] that was not scientifically explainable."

Robert concluded his lengthy letter to me philosophically. "I have often wondered what I saw on that morning. There I was, sleeping in the bedroom that my parents had slept in many years ago, in the home that my father had taken such pride in building. Was it a final visit in some form from the spirit of my father, a man I loved and respected? It's one more question I wish to have answered in the hereafter."

Clocks May Not Be Coo-coo

Many circumstances can increase the chances of a conversation about ghosts. People whose electrical appliances mysteriously malfunction, those who experience inexplicable cold spots or drafts in a room, or clock-owners whose timepieces operate in strange ways may mention these events. And, of course, the approach of October 31, Halloween, always increases the number of ghost stories heard and told.

During the afternoon of Halloween 1997, I was invited to be a guest on the CBC radio program "Midday Express." Listeners phoned in and told us about paranormal experiences they'd had. Predictably, people were talking about cold spots, washing machines that seemingly had minds of their own and other sorts of ghostly activity.

Clocks and the supernatural often seem to be connected.

Then Elizabeth phoned recalling a whimsical incident of a spirit manifesting through a clock.

Calling from Edmonton, Elizabeth explained that after her grandfather died, she stayed the night with her mother to make sure the older woman would be all right. When they arrived home they noticed an unfamiliar light "coming out of" a pendulum clock that had belonged to the family for years. Elizabeth explained that the light then moved and "went out the window. The next morning, the clock was lying on its side."

As nothing like that had ever happened before and has not happened since, Elizabeth has always wondered if her grandfather's spirit moving from one level of existence to another had something to do with the bizarre activity of the clock.

Final Contact

A man named Bill called Margie Taylor's CBC phone-in show on one of the days when I was the guest and the topic was ghosts. He was in his truck out near Morley while he was telling us this delightful tale of activity from the afterlife.

Bill explained that although he is now middle-aged, these ghostly events took place in the late 1960s when he was 12. The enigma concerned a clock that Bill's grandfather had owned. The timepiece was old, at least 70 years old even then. Although the clock never functioned, Bill's grandfather was extremely fond of it.

"He always talked about fixing this clock but never got around to it," Bill recalled. "After he died, his bedroom door was locked. The family got together about a week later and when we were all sitting around in the kitchen, all of a sudden we heard this 'bong, bong, bong.'"

Bill paused before continuing to describe his memories of the supernatural event that occurred that day. "It was very strange. Everybody was just sitting there. The looks on everyone's faces were of disbelief. For me, only 12 years old, it was very dramatic and I had this chill go down my spine. I had never felt like that before."

The adults knew that the sounds emanating from the deceased's bedroom had to be investigated. "They opened the locked door and looked at the clock. The pendulum was moving back and forth. It was just unbelievable, especially as, even now, I'm not one who believes in things like that."

Tentatively, the relatives of the recently deceased man approached the strangely behaving clock and stilled its pendulum, perhaps hoping that their action would put an end to the phenomenon of what they believed to be the deceased grandfather's presence remaining among them.

Not too many days later, Bill's mother and grand-mother went to a fortune teller and told him about the clock. "The fortune teller became really excited and offered them any price for the clock. He also told them not to stop the clock," apparently for fear of breaking any "kind of spiritual connection."

The two women did not listen to the fortune teller's advice—they did not give up their beloved relative's clock nor did they ever try to start the pendulum swinging again in an attempt to restore a possible link with the spirit world. To Bill's knowledge, his grandfather's presumed manifestation through his beloved clock was the only time after the man's death that he returned to those he had lived with and loved.

Husband's Presence Still Felt

Jokes about difficult relations between women and their mothers-in-law are legion, but the tone of Carla's letter to me about her mother-in-law's recent experience showed that this family does not have such problems. Because the events recorded here are highly personal, all the names have been altered. The family's real names are, of course, on file.

Carla began, "My father-in-law, Art, passed away last June [2000]. He was out mowing his lawn and collapsed. My mother-in-law found him in the yard when she went out to call him for dinner." Carla added that his passing was very sudden and left a terrible void in her mother-in-law's life. "[She] was very dependent on Art for many things and he was very set in his ways."

"A few weeks after he passed away," Carla continued, "I went over to her house for a visit. We were chatting in the living room when I noted that the clock on the mantle had stopped. As Mom has bad arthritis, I offered to wind it for her. She was sad and said, 'No,' that Art had always done it and that the clock was finicky and Art always told her to let him wind it. I think she felt sentimental and asked that I leave it alone."

Carla, of course, abided by the recently widowed woman's wishes, but added, "that evening I relayed this story to my husband, who stated that he had also noted the clock and had offered to wind it on a visit he had with her several days before." Apparently the bereaved woman refused that offer too.

"Then my husband turned to me and asked, 'Did you happen to notice the time' [the clock was stopped at]?" Carla recalled.

Carla hadn't noticed, but her husband had. "It had stopped at twenty to six. That is the time that Mom found Dad in the yard. She specifically noted that."

Chapter 4

Ghosts in Public

Is it possible that, as we go about our daily lives,

we may unknowingly be encountering ghosts?

Pool's Overflowing— With Ghosts!

No sooner had my book *More Ghost Stories of Alberta* been released in 1996 than the employees of a public swimming pool in Edmonton's southside called me with their story. Few tales of hauntings are worth waiting five years to tell, but this story, surely, is one of those few. Better still, the staff members who spoke with me implied that discussions with their colleagues at other pools suggested there might be more wet wraiths around swimming pools than anyone ever suspected.

The legend of this haunting goes back at least 20 years. Emily, as the ghost of the little girl has been named, is the most mischievous of the resident spirits. Perhaps because this spirit is so child-like and non-threatening there is no record of anyone ever feeling afraid of Emily. She likes to run about the premises playing, giggling and calling out staff members' names. When the employees round a corner to see who called them, they find the area the voice came from is empty.

One of the least desirable, but most necessary, jobs around any swimming pool is keeping the toilets clean. Emily even tries to bring a bit of levity to that chore. When the employee assigned to the toilet-cleaning task starts to work, the playful spirit will often turn on the faucets in the sinks more than a metre away.

Beach balls stored in a wire bin against a wall have suddenly flown out of their container to bounce around the pool deck. Such events are especially unnerving to those employees working alone either before or after the pool opens, and workers have occasionally been driven out of the building by ghostly hijinks. Generally, after a few deep breaths of fresh air, the employee is able to go back into the haunted building and continue with the work.

Some staff members have fallen into the habit of talking to the little girl's spirit as they work. They're more comfortable talking to the spirit than working their entire shift with a nagging feeling of being closely followed while not being able to see who or what is tagging along at their heels.

Emily does occasionally allow herself to be seen. Once, when the building was locked and only one employee was on duty, the top of a little girl's head was seen bobbing up the ramp past the cashier's wicket. The child's spirit may even once have allowed her image to be captured in a photograph, as a strange and inexplicable image showed up in a picture taken near the cashier's office.

Once during public swimming hours, two lifeguards were on deck. One guard was trying, unsuccessfully, to get the other's attention because a swimmer had developed a nosebleed. The first guard watched in amazement as her co-worker walked along the deck, into and out of a white cloud or haze of vapours. To this day both guards wonder if the foggy formation was actually Emily also trying, in her ghostly way, to draw the other guard's attention to the swimmer who required assistance.

The staff is also sure about another ghost, whom they call Hank. He haunts the pool's filter room and, although he too has been seen, he's more frequently smelled. Hank apparently exudes a distinctly masculine odour which, oddly, some describe as like a man's cologne while others say the smell is like that of a man who's been doing intense physical work. Like Emily, Hank sometimes manifests as a patch of cloudy air, but his image has also been seen clearly enough that a witness was able to describe the thin-striped coveralls he was wearing.

A phantom sound that bothers most of the employees at this pool is the sound of someone running his or her hand along the railing that runs up the ramp from the change rooms into the pool area. Several guards and maintenance workers have heard the sound when they know for a fact that they were alone in a locked building at the time. The sound is so convincing that employees will repeatedly call out to who-ever might have come in, but, of course, there's never any answer because no other human being is in the building.

Whatever presence creates the sound on the railing may also be the one responsible for causing echoes of phantom footfalls, but my informants were adamant that such heavy steps are distinctly different from the clicking sounds of high-heeled shoes heard in the gymnasium of the school attached to the pool.

Other phantom sounds in the gymnasium include the clanging noises that free weights make when they bang together. The room those sounds come from used to be a weight room, but it hadn't been used as such for several years by the time those sounds were heard. This racket is most commonly heard at night. It is also during night shifts that sourceless shadows are occasionally seen under doors.

Like most people who work in haunted buildings, the employees at this pool have developed "antennae" for when the spirits are around. "The air gets heavy," one woman told me. "The feeling is very different" when one or other of the ghosts is present, said another.

To gather clues about the identity of their resident spirits, one of the long-time staff members visited the City Archives. Archival aerial photographs taken as early as the mid-1920s showed that a race track once existed in that approximate area as did an "auto court" (the forerunner of a recreation vehicle campground). Neither piece of information was really much help in the search for the ghosts' identities.

Any suspicions that pool employees are sensing ghosts because they work in close proximity to some powerful chemicals are put to rest by the fact that Emily has been known to have some fun at the expense of tradespeople called in to do temporary work. Two electricians had been working together for some time when one left the area to go to the washroom. While he was there he heard the distinct sound of a little girl's giggle and at the same time, his partner, still on the job, saw a sourceless shadow. At the same time, the dial of the radio they'd been listening to moved from a rock station to one that broadcast vintage rock and roll tunes. When they heard noises just around a corner, the pair went to investigate. There, they distinctly saw the outline of a little girl who they estimated was about 11 or 12 years of age. By that time, the electricians had witnessed considerably more than they'd been prepared for. They packed up and left for the night.

Given the number of years the ghosts have been associated with that swimming pool, it's unlikely that they will be leaving anytime soon. In addition to a full complement of loyal lifeguards, some swimming pools apparently have even longer lasting afterlife guards.

Securing the Security System

When Nancy met Bill, the news made the front page of the *Calgary Herald*. For good reason. This was far from a regular "boy meets girl" story, for Nancy is Nancy Sterling, then manager of membership services at Calgary's chamber of commerce, and Bill is the ghost who haunts the chamber's building.

In the May 14, 2000, edition of the *Herald,* Nancy Sterling explained that the meeting occurred one evening when she'd decided to work late. She was by herself at her desk when she was surprised to hear the sound of the drawers of a nearby filing cabinet opening and closing. Curious and a bit startled, Nancy peeked out of her office and looked toward the area where the filing cabinets stood. Not only was one drawer now open but, impossibly, two stood open. If the laws of physics were to be obeyed, a filing cabinet with two drawers open should have tipped over from imbalance. Nancy didn't know what to make of what she saw. She did know, however, that she was not about to hang around and investigate. She immediately dropped what she'd been doing and headed for home.

Nancy is not the only one to have had strange experiences in the building. Those who have had ghostly encounters suspect that the spirit is that of a recently deceased man named Bill who had been at the chamber of commerce offices frequently as he was responsible for maintaining the building's security system.

In the mid-1990s, when Bill was only 35, he died of a heart attack. The staff was saddened at his parting and also concerned about the future of the security system's repairs because it had always seemed that Bill had just the right touch when odd things happened to the alarms. Such worries were unfounded, however, as there have been remarkably few problems with the equipment since the man's death, far fewer than during his life.

This situation seems to support the suspicions of some people connected with the chamber of commerce offices that the building was haunted even before Bill's death and that the original ghost was causing the troubles that frequently brought Bill to the job site. Now, these same folks theorize, Bill has come back to the building he tended so loyally in life to protect it from the original troublemaking ghost.

The identity of *that* phantom can only be guessed at because the building has had a long and colourful past, but it is clear that the Centre Street South office is definitely well haunted. An invisible presence occasionally not only operates the elevator, but also is heard to get on and off it. Once, a section of sliding wall moved, apparently of its own volition, effectively trapping the workers in that area. Unexplained tapping sounds occur, doors open and close when no one is near them and, in classic ghostly form, lights turn on and off when no one is near the switches.

Although Nancy Sterling has gone on to other employment challenges, many of her former colleagues, including Bill, continue to labour on in the haunted Calgary chamber of commerce building.

Who Patrols the Police?

Lacombe, Alberta, on Highway 12 just north of Red Deer, is as pretty a little town as one could hope to find. It was one of several Alberta towns that participated in a downtown revitalization project known as the Main Street Programme, having its downtown core recreated to look like it did in the early 1900s. It is so picturesque and looks so idyllic that you'd wonder if the citizens even needed a police department. Apparently they do, though, if for no other reason than to patrol whatever's present in the police station.

Joy Timothy explained: "In 1990, I was working for the Lacombe Police Service. I was employed as a part-time dispatcher. I worked mainly night shifts from 7 PM to 7 AM. The building we worked in was quite old and we shared it with the Fire Department. It was a wedged-shaped, two-storey place. The bottom floor held the dispatch office, the main working area for the members, the cells and a small coffee area. The police and fire vehicle bays were off the cell area. The top floor consisted of a long hallway, with two or three offices and a conference room."

Joy continued her description by explaining that "whenever anyone walked down the hallway you could hear a very distinctive noise of footsteps and a loud creaking as each step was taken."

Such a creaky old building might not be conducive to catching a nap between calls, but at least anyone downstairs would know when there was someone upstairs—maybe. Joy began to suspect that all was not normal in the building:

"On several occasions, around two o'clock in the morning, I would smell an overpowering scent of cut flowers. This happened numerous times during the winter months when the windows were all shut tight and there was no possible explanation for the smell."

Although she was never able to track down the source of the fragrance, the experiences did prepare her for the ghostly action that was ahead for her.

"One night I was on shift alone with just one constable who was out on patrol. It was around 2 or 2:30 AM when I heard the distinct sound of someone fairly heavy walking along the hallway upstairs. I called the constable on the radio and asked him to return to the station. He went upstairs and checked all over. There was no one there, and the doors were secure. He left the office again, and within a few minutes I heard the same pounding of footsteps along the hall and the scent of cut flowers was almost sickening. I called him again to come in. He was still right outside the station, so it only took him a matter of seconds to come back in. I asked him just to wait a while to see if the footsteps would happen again."

The pair didn't have long to wait before the phantom footsteps once again marched their way across the upstairs floor. "The constable heard the sounds too. He took a heavy flashlight with him upstairs and searched everywhere. There was no one there and the doors were still secure."

As there didn't seem much else to do, the pair waited out their shift by attending to their duties. Joy added, "In the morning I discussed with my supervisor what had been happening and she said one of the other dispatchers had also experienced the same kinds of things over the years. I talked to this other dispatcher and found we had just about identical experiences with the scent of flowers and the pounding footsteps at around the same time— between 2 and 3 AM.

The answer to the ghostly enigma no doubt lies buried somewhere in the history of the building. At least the noisy spirit's presence does not seem to be anything to fear.

Holy Ghosts

All his life, Dan Gibson (a pseudonym) has been closely associated with a mainstream Protestant Church. He contacted me after reading one of my previous ghost story books and finding that he could relate to many of the instances people had recounted to me for that book.

Dan began our conversation by explaining that, as a youngster, he'd had a great deal of difficulty coming to terms with his paranormal experiences. "It was hard, because growing up in the household that I did, I was taught that ghosts just don't exist."

Eventually, though, the strength and reality of Dan's encounters contradicted that teaching. "I know that I pick up on things. I've always felt this but I can never predict when it's going to happen."

Fittingly, two of Dan's most dramatic encounters occurred in churches. The first took place in the late 1970s, in a then-rundown section of Calgary. Dan explained that he attended a Christian school and was friends with the daughter of a church leader. "Her father had asked her to go over [to the church] and pick something up from his office. We went into the church and I immediately got very uneasy feelings. We were walking through the basement of the church and the light behind us went out. We turned around and it came back on. We knew we were the only [flesh-and-blood] ones there but there was noise and a lot of sounds of someone walking around upstairs."

Not surprisingly, the two youngsters beat a hasty retreat from the spooky subterranean depths, but they did not leave the church property. As with many churches, this one had a hall built on to it. "I walked into the hall. There was a picture of a man hanging on the wall," Dan recalled. "I swear to you, I looked at this picture and said, 'He hates me.' This was a picture of a very angry man. His eyes just burned out of the picture."

Although it was certainly not one of his favourite childhood memories, Dan never forgot that experience. As an adult, he learned that lights turning on and off, phantom sounds, a feeling of hatred and uncomfortably eerie sensations are generally acknowledged to be elements of a haunting, but at the time he was shocked and frightened. Worse, the paranormal influence was having a widespread detrimental effect on the congregation. Almost everyone associated with this parish had been adversely affected by the wrathful resident wraith.

"My friend's dad was on the verge of a nervous breakdown, the people in the church were really starting to get angry with each other but they didn't know why. There wasn't any particular issue," Dan told me.

Despite the denomination's general denial of all things metaphysical, "they brought in an outside team of church people interested in looking for spirits and that sort of thing. They only lasted till about 1 AM before they were out of there. It was awful, apparently. There were thumpings and flashing lights. Whatever it was knew it was being hunted and it accelerated its activities."

That was when the church called in its own expert, whom we shall refer to by the initial of his first name, 'G.'

"G went into a back storage room and found a wolf's head on a stick. It was from a former cub pack. It was stuffed and mounted. There was a black cloud or a mist going around it, circling it like a planet does the sun. He took the wolf's head out and burned it. He sprinkled the whole church with holy water." The exorcism was apparently a success, for Dan reported that they "didn't really have a problem again."

Dan did add, however, that in his late teens he was back in the hall attached to the church "and that picture was still there. It's still an evil picture." At that time, Dan was mature enough to be told by G that the man in the picture "used to hit kids with a cane. He didn't like children and he would swipe at them with a cane."

And what about the church itself? "When I went back in there for a youth group that would meet at that church I still felt something. It wasn't as powerful but it was still really annoyed. The force was just, in some way, restrained. If I went back there and walked into that hall today, if that picture was still there, I know I'd get the same feeling. Still to this day, even driving by the place I look away. It has a very dark, extremely heavy atmosphere." Perhaps in that Calgary church, an echo of the previous haunting lingers for the most sensitive to discern.

Dan had a similar experience in a different church in the mid-1980s when he was in Banff with a youth group.

"We were going to be staying overnight and sleeping in the church. I was about 14. This was when I was still a little unsure of my ability to sense things but I knew something was in there. I freaked out. I could walk in [to the church] but the idea of sleeping in there, no way. That just wasn't going to happen. I ended up sleeping in the van in the parking lot," Dan remembered and added that the difficulty of his decision was compounded by the inevitable peer pressure that one feels at that age. "Everyone was asking, 'What's wrong with you? What's wrong with you?'"

Despite Dan's desire to be included in the group and to avoid the discomfort of sleeping in the van, he was not able to make himself spend the night in the church. Again, he didn't fully understand his aversion to the place at the time and it wasn't until he was involved with the church in a more mature capacity and met G again that he finally learned what his perceptive nature had responded to.

"G explained it to me this way. The way the church was built you go in the front door and the secretary's office is off to one side. You have to go past her office to get into the church proper. What was happening was this old man was going through the door. He would keep on going. The first couple of times the secretary yelled at the man. He didn't react or say anything, so finally she got fed up with it. When she saw him next, she jumped up from her desk and ran up after him. He just kept on going down the aisle. He turned right and he was gone. He walked right [through] a wall."

The secretary stared in amazement. This was the same image she'd seen walk into the church on numerous occasions. Now at least she knew why he didn't answer her. He may have looked like a man, but by then he was a ghost.

Dan concluded, "They phoned G. He came and did an exorcism and that took care of it."

Today, Dan is an adult, and his association with the church is even stronger than it was when he was a boy. Fortunately for his peace of mind, his understanding of his enhanced sensory powers is also stronger, so he is much more comfortable with his special abilities.

Haunted Hospitals

The Calgary General Hospital has been gone for many years now—imploded by a skillfully and precisely set blast. However, stories about the ghosts that haunted the old place have not settled as quickly as the dustcloud from the demolition.

Carolyn Vacey was a nurse in the Intensive Care Unit (ICU) of the General. In a lengthy and thoughtful letter, Carolyn shared details of some of the "strange ghostly happenings" that she had experienced over the years she worked in the old hospital. Carolyn began by explaining that the Coronary Care Unit (CCU) and a Trauma Unit were two specialty areas within the ICU. They were separated by only a hall, yet the majority of the phantom activity that this nurse knew of was restricted to the Coronary Care section, especially a "double room," numbered Rooms 8 and 9.

"Often, in the morning after a night shift, when only one patient was occupying the room, the nurse would go

Before it was demolished, this hospital was the site of many ghostly experiences.

in to assess that patient before shift change. The patient would say they had a fine night and that the man in the next bed kept them company and covered them up when their blankets fell back," Carolyn recalled.

Although the nurse was, of course, pleased that the patient had been comfortable throughout the night, that satisfaction was always mixed with concern because there had been no other patient in the room. Stranger still was that "even women patients seemed comforted by this 'man' and did not seem distressed in the least that there was a man in the room with them."

Rooms 8 and 9 were also where heart monitors would turn on—"always on the night shift!" Carolyn recalled—even if there was no patient in either of the beds. "This would never happen in any other room. The nurses would go in and turn them off, only to have them turn on again later. You could see the room while sitting at the [nurses'] desk so no one could be sneaking in there to do it. These monitors could only be manually turned on from in the rooms, although there was a central monitor at the desk, which was how we could see that they were on."

"One night nurse was alone in CCU and she noted the monitor [was turned] on in Room 8." Presumably this nurse was aware of the enigma associated with that space, for Carolyn emphasized that the woman "reluctantly went in, turned [the monitor] off and came back to the desk to find her coffee spilled and her papers strewn all over the desk. There was no one else in CCU."

By that point in her letter, Carolyn Vacey had certainly captured my attention!

Carolyn concluded her note to me by relating an incident experienced by a co-worker named Andrea. "One day, while working on the Trauma side of the ICU, [Andrea] heard the 'help' button go off in CCU. Andrea ran into CCU to the room of a patient who was in cardiac arrest. The nurse in CCU had got the 'crash cart' [a small gurney stocked with all the drugs and machines necessary to deal with a cardiac arrest] and Andrea quickly defibrillated [sent electric currents through the heart to temporarily stop all activity with the goal of having the heart beat restart itself at a normal pace] the patient by using paddles on the chest."

Carolyn explained that by this time, "the rest of the 'code team' was then present" and Andrea's responsibilities were, therefore, over. The quick-responding nurse returned to her regular post in the Trauma area and remained there. At some point later in her shift she was told the good news that the patient had recovered.

"A couple of days later, Andrea was on duty again, this time working on CCU. Breakfast trays arrived and Andrea went in to the resuscitated man's room and greeted him 'Good morning.' She introduced herself and he replied, 'Oh, I know who you are. You are the nurse who put the paddles on my chest and gave me electricity.' When Andrea asked 'Who told you that?' he replied, 'No one, I was watching you from up there!' and he pointed to the ceiling."

It would seem that during the emergency situation, the patient's spirit had left his corporeal body and been an observer to the successful lifesaving attempts going on.

Charlie's Story

Not all hospitals are demolished when their terms as efficient health care centres end. Some, like the old Holy Cross Hospital in Calgary, are renovated in order to fulfill other useful, often health-care related, purposes. It would seem, at least from the following story, that while the living beings associated with the Holy Cross Hospital all left the building before the makeover began, at least one ethereal being did not.

Jane Allan, then a student at the new Massage Therapy Training Institute, wrote to me about some very strange encounters she'd been part of and others she had been told of.

"Just before we were to enter the new clinic, we were standing in a very small and empty room. Actually, it was more of an empty space than a room. There were only three of us but it felt like I was standing in the middle of an overcrowded room. I could almost hear conversations echoing between unseen individuals. I felt sardined between people, although no one [but the three of us] was in sight," Jane described. "I got the feeling that the crowd of individuals sensed me, but they kept talking amongst themselves. It wasn't scary at all."

Her lack of fright became important when Jane realized she would have occasion to be in that empty-yet-over-crowded room often. "Every time I go back to that room I get the same feeling." As she makes her way away from the room, however, "the feeling and echoes disappear."

In addition to that invisible crowd, "there is also a 'star' ghost. His name is Charlie. I have spoken to two security guards and they have told me Charlie's story."

Jane explained, "Charlie was a patient at the Holy Cross. Nobody knows what he died of or when, just that [his ghost] is still there. Every evening at 11 o'clock, Charlie appears. He loves to whistle, but can't carry a tune, which causes him to whistle off key. He enjoys walking the halls in the basement of the hospital. When renovations were being made to accommodate the new school, some work-ers met Charlie. One story was that there were two plumbers who were working a few feet away from each other. I guess Charlie manifested in front of one of the men and the other heard Charlie whistling."

Demonstrating an admirable command of understate-ment, Jane added, "This frightened them and they left for home early."

Despite the unnerving working conditions, these men did have an obligation to fulfill, so "the next day, the men returned but with a radio. Charlie didn't [appear]. Maybe

*Even after this hospital was converted into a training institute,
spirits roamed the halls.*

he heard the song he whistles and realized he was off key."

Bringing radios to work turned out to be an effective
way of keeping the spirit at bay. "Every time someone
brought a radio to the work site, Charlie stayed away."

Jane's curiosity evidently wasn't as easy to control. She
explained, "I have looked at a section of the basement
through a window in a door. It was a long hallway. As I
gazed around, a shadow fell upon the floor and moved from
one wall to the next. There was no one visible there, but
something had caused that shadow. At first I felt welcomed,
almost as if Charlie himself was greeting me [at] his home,
but within a few seconds, I felt sheer terror. Something else
was there with me. It felt … evil. I turned to my friend …
and told her I had to run back upstairs. She didn't question
me, just followed my lead."

Since that frightening occasion Jane has had the
opportunity to reflect upon her experience that day.
"Whatever it was down there made the air so heavy and
dense. It almost seemed as if my feet were glued to the

ground. My running back up the stairs was partly done by myself and partly by some unseen force, almost as if I was carried up the stairs by an invisible hand. Whoever or whatever it was—I thank [it]."

For Charlie, anyway, it would seem that he's simply continuing to function in his reality while our reality whirls around him at what used to be the Holy Cross Hospital.

Spectre in the Corridors

A chronic care hospital in Edmonton was rumoured to be haunted even when I was associated with the facility in the early 1980s. Like many hospitals, this one included a series of basement tunnels. A man named Keith, who worked a full-time evening job on the main floor of the hospital, told me that he always felt extremely uncomfortable when he had to be in those subterranean corridors. He didn't have any idea what caused this unusual feeling until a co-worker explained that local lore indicated this area of the building was said to be haunted by a woman who was once the head of the hospital's housekeeping department. She apparently liked to "take advantage" of the young men under her supervision, physically grabbing at them. Through the years, her aggression, the men's fear of what might happen to their employment futures and their repulsion at her blatant overtures combined to leave the place haunted by the vibrations of the conflicting emotional tensions.

Once Keith heard the history of those hallways, he knew what it was that he had been feeling. In addition to sensing the detritus of horror experienced by the young men of generations ago, he had also been made uncomfortable by the sensation that the department head's evil hand was reaching out across time—to him.

Another informant indicates that a friend who worked in the facility and remembers it when it was an active care hospital "swears she has seen several World War I soldiers and past patients," even "a patient she knew when she was younger."

"The ghosts seem to congregate in the basement [where several] areas have been closed off, for instance, the morgue and an area once used for electroshock treatments," according to my correspondent whose identity I have on file. With that kind of a history, it's not too surprising that there is considerable negative energy recorded in that one area of the hospital.

Nursing Writer

A student of mine from the days when I taught writing-related courses was a registered nurse who had chosen to work on a casual basis in order to devote as much time as possible to developing her writing career. One of the hospitals she took occasional shifts in was another chronic care hospital—this one just north of Edmonton.

On May 23, 1999, this woman, whom I will call Doreen, began working a series of overnight shifts. "After the third night I began to pick up some vibes around the place. I thought I was getting a little too sleep-deprived [because] when I was looking out over one of the old buildings, built in the 1940s or some such, I kept seeing a strange light flicker in a window and some shadows going back and forth."

This might not have struck Doreen as being too unusual except that she had been told that the building she was looking at had been closed down and therefore was completely empty. A bit concerned by the conflict of what she knew she was seeing versus what she knew she'd been told, Doreen found another employee, one with more experience at the hospital. In order that the other woman not think she was strange, Doreen tried to make light of what she'd seen.

"I made a joke about seeing a ghost. She [the other employee] didn't bat an eye, but said, 'Oh yes, some other staff have said they've seen ghosts of some sort out there too.'"

At least Doreen now knew that what she was seeing was not caused by the fact that she was overtired.

During a night shift about a month later, Doreen slipped outside to have a cigarette. Doreen explained, "The door opens out to the main entrance ... the staff put a chair and an ashtray there ... I opened the door to the outside to let some air in. There was a door to a storage closet behind me and it was rattling. I figured it was just the wind ... a breeze shaking this door, so I tried to adjust my chair against this door to settle down the rattling."

Much to Doreen's concern, this move, which should have fixed the problem, "did not help." Slowly, she began to become aware, in a broader sense, of her surroundings. Seconds later, she realized that the rattling door should have been still even without a chair propped up against it because "there was no wind."

She "scuttled back to the unit" with a "strange feeling," convinced that the rattling door had been caused by "another ghost trying to get out."

Or, of course, it could have been ghosts trying to get Doreen out of *their* domain. If this was the case, then the closet phantoms' methods were successful.

One spirit whose identity is known was never a patient in that hospital but a student nurse. Legend has it that, during her period of training, the young woman killed herself. Even today, her apparition can be seen wandering about the hospital grounds.

Considering the psychic trauma, and of course, the deaths associated with hospitals, it is not much of a surprise that so many of them are homes to restless spirits.

Haunted Hallowed Halls

When I first began to collect ghost stories, I kept hearing rumours that the University of Alberta campus had a history of being haunted. After some concentrated effort, combined with a bit of good luck, I've pinned down at least some of the stories associated with buildings in and around the campus in Edmonton.

The first story does not actually take place on the university grounds but in a nearby house—a house so close to the campus that it is always occupied by students. One of those occupants spoke about the haunting to an *Edmonton Journal* reporter. She described hearing the eerie sounds of a man's angry voice, a woman's voice pleading for mercy and a child's plaintive cries. When the background of the house was investigated, it was learned that, in the mid-1930s, an unhappy family had lived there. One night, after the man had been drinking heavily, he killed his wife in a fit of jealousy. Minutes later, he also killed the baby, and then took his own life. It would seem that those horrific deeds have left the house in a permanently haunted state.

On campus there's a considerably more benign ghost. Corbett Hall is one of the oldest buildings at the University of Alberta. It is located near the southern boundary of the campus itself and is home to the ghost of Emily. Her presence is so well accepted by the administration of the school that she was even acknowledged in the alumni magazine, *New Trail*. It is thought that Emily dates back to the time when Corbett Hall was a teacher-training centre, or what was called a Normal School then, and that Emily was a student there. Emily's spirit is pleasant, but, in life, she must have felt a great attachment to the place where her soul has remained, for she can still be seen walking across the stage in the building's auditorium. No one knows whether her spirit is eternally striding out to receive her teaching certificate or perhaps making her entrance for a school play.

Also on campus, Ring House One, located near the northwestern boundary of the campus, is now occupied by the university's department of museums and collections services. Many years ago, however, it was home to Dr. and Mrs. Robert Newton during his tenure as president of the university. Many people are convinced that the spirit of Mrs. Newton—Emma Reid Newton—has never left her former home. She's said to turn lights on and off as needed by those working in the area and has been blamed for moving objects from one place to another.

A woman I spoke with at length informed me that she had been involved in a meeting on the second floor of Ring House One. When the group she was a part of suddenly felt a gust of wind come up the stairs, one of the people went downstairs to close the front door, which they presumed someone must have left open. The door was found not only to be closed, but also locked—just as it had been after the last person entered the building sometime earlier. A search of the main floor proved that no one was there, and the previously felt gust of wind could not be accounted for.

Shortly after that rather unnerving occurrence, the meeting concluded and my informant was eventually left alone with just one student. As the pair chatted and prepared to leave, they were shocked to hear what sounded like a roll of paper being laid out. They searched the entire premises but found nothing to account for the sound they'd both heard so distinctly. My informant wondered if the ghost of Emma Newton was possibly setting up to decorate a room in her house with wallpaper! Perhaps we'll never know because the woman told me that she and her companion fled at that point, convinced that they'd attended a meeting in a haunted house, possibly with one more participant than had been acknowledged.

Not far to the east of Ring House is HUB Mall, a unique combination of residences and retail shops. In at least one particular spot, HUB is also haunted. Apparently, there's a pillar of cold air running up through the building—in exactly the location where a haunted house once stood. The house was torn down to make room for the newer, multi-purpose, building. But, not all former occupants may have vacated the premises.

Some years ago, I had the pleasure of meeting one of the people who'd been raised in that now demolished haunted house. She said that everyone in her family accepted the ghost's presence, but she would not discuss the details. The ghost, my informant implied, was something of a family favourite, and she felt that telling me about the haunting would be tantamount to gossiping about someone without their permission! As my informant is also a writer, perhaps one day she'll write about her family's paranormal home life herself.

The most heartwarming of all the legends from the University of Alberta campus indicates that starting on November 11, 1939, and all during World War II, the pump organ in Convocation Hall in the Old Arts Building would sound the taps melody each night, even though no one that anyone could see was anywhere near the keyboard. As Convocation Hall is dedicated to those associated with the University who fought in the wars, the story is absolutely fitting.

Another story involving the University of Alberta is that of the haunted mummy case that apparently lost its spirit upon its transfer from a museum in St. Albert. In 1985, when the musée heritage first opened, Michael Tymchuk was the facility's director. When he found that a well-travelled couple in the city just north of Edmonton "had been using a mummy-filled coffin as a coffee table in their living room," he was intrigued. When he managed to obtain it for the new museum's opening, he was delighted.

He had the artifact transferred and examined. The coffin encased the mummified body of a 27-year-old man who had apparently worked as a scribe before succumbing to cancer. This information was written up and placed on display along with the mummy.

Tymchuk's delight, however, apparently turned to horror when, according to an article in a St. Albert newspaper, "Tymchuk, accompanied by a security guard, was reading the information out loud when both men heard a voice." As they were alone in a locked building, both men presumed that the phantom voice was connected with the display, and the men raced each other to the exit.

Kathleen Popiel from St. Albert explained, "After the incident, the security guard refused to walk the museum rounds and found other employment."

Once the display was transferred to the university, no sound was ever again heard from it—at least none has been reported!

According to the *Calgary Herald*, the University of Calgary is not a ghost-free zone. The phantom of the Earth Sciences Building is presumed to be a former Dean of Women Students. Mrs. Fish was associated with the university during the 1950s when it was a satellite campus of the University of Alberta. She apparently died prematurely. Her spirit is blamed for strange sounds and doors that slam by themselves. For those who might think that the spectre of Mrs. Fish is being wrongly accused, rest assured that the woman's image *has* been seen, and recognized.

The Old Partridge Hill School

The kind lady who shared this story with me pointedly did *not* mention any names in her retelling. In order to respect her generosity and privacy I have replicated her story exactly as she related it to me.

I experienced this apparition (in 1991) in a very old schoolhouse that was transformed into a nice comfortable home ... owned by our son and his wife in Partridge Hill. They had their first son and were expecting their second son.

When we came over for a visit it was always an invitation to stay overnight. We slept in an east bedroom, a guest room. One time we came for a visit and stayed overnight. My husband was already sound asleep and I was still awake. I couldn't believe what I was hearing, a rhythmical tapping on the window. I got up and looked to see if there was anything hanging near the window or on the outside, but nothing was visible. (I had heard it at other times when we had slept there.) The tapping continued, three taps, a pause. I thought, *Well, I don't see anything, so I will just tell my husband the next day.* He could check it out more carefully in the morning. Soon I drifted into sleep and when I awoke in the morning, the tapping was gone. Together with my husband we walked on the outside and I explained about the tapping. There was nothing near that window that could have caused that tapping and we left for home.

We returned a few weeks later to stay with our son and young grandson. It was the first week in April 1991. Now the guest room was made into the nursery for the baby. The beds were removed and the crib was put in. My husband and I moved into the spare bedroom. A strange feeling of undisclosed presence seemed to be around me. Somehow the former tapping instances were always on my mind. As I prepared to go to bed, as usual I prayed and thanked God for the baby's safe arrival and all our daily blessings. Then I assumed someone was asking for extra prayers or had some special needs and might, in some way, let me know. Soon I drifted into some dimension where I was neither asleep nor awake, it's hard to describe. However, this vision appeared—a tall, broad-shouldered man in a wide-striped suit, seemed like the colour was either navy or black. He had high cheekbones, his hair was dark black and combed slick, straight back. The shirt was white and a different style with somewhat of a high collar; the shoes were black patent leather. All in all, he was dressed like a professional person. He was standing in the doorway of the room we were sleeping in. He looked down upon us as we lay on that air mattress on the floor that we were sleeping on. He smiled but did not speak and was gone. I was not afraid or in anyway disturbed; actually I was amazed to have had this vision and that I could be so calm and collected.

Even now, years later it still comes to my mind. I decided to write it up, as it was rather an unusual event in my life. My [son and his] family have moved on as there were other strange occurrences and unusual happenings in the old school yard.

Judging from my delightful correspondent's experiences in the former schoolhouse, my guess is that either a long-deceased teacher or a school principal was merely continuing to keep an eye on what used to be his domain.

Retail Wraith

While a successful retail establishment operates around it, a spirit lives out its afterlife in a northwest Calgary building. For the staff, the realization that they were working in a haunted place came about gradually. A former employee named Susan remembered that as far back as 1994, one of her co-workers used to maintain that there was a ghost in the place. He would make this comment whenever "something was out of place or there was a strange noise."

Initially, the man's co-workers merely chuckled at his paranormal theory, but then "one by one every member of the staff had some sort of bizarre experience that just could not be laughed off," Susan explained. "All of us would 'see' something in our peripheral vision. Thinking it was a customer, one of us would 'hit the floor' to make a sale, but there was never anyone where we thought they should be."

Susan is a pragmatic sort who was willing to make allowances for such oddities. "Seeing things in one's peripheral vision is not too strange. It was just that it happened to all of us so often."

Susan stated ominously that although no one realized it at the time, "things were going to get stranger. I was working alone one night near Christmas time. I was making up some Christmas trays and baskets. The aisle I was in had a display of birdhouses and feeders attached by rope to the cross sections of the false ceilings. They had always been displayed there without a problem. I had my head down and was working away when some movement caught my eye. The birdhouses were swinging slowly to and fro. As I watched they began to swing harder and harder."

Susan's reaction to the phenomenon was decisive: "I left my work where it was and grabbed my coat and keys. I could not get out of there fast enough."

Susan was certainly not the only one to have an unnerving experience with an invisible force in the store.

"One of the clerks always wore an apron when he worked. Several times he felt someone (or something) tug at the apron. He would turn to see who was trying to get his attention but there was no one around," the young woman recalled before adding that, not surprisingly, "he was more than a little rattled."

Susan continued, "The manager of the shop came to work early one morning and made his usual rounds, checking doors and flicking on the warehouse lights."

All was as it should have been until "he heard a radio in the office come on and the very distinctive sound of a woman's high-heeled shoes on the tile floor. The office can be accessed by a back door, and often is, by two of the women who work there."

Presuming that one of his staff had also decided to come to work early, the manager made his way into the office area. "There was absolutely no one there," Susan stated. "He looked all over the shop. He knew for certain that the radio was not on when he came in but [now] it was blaring away. The poor guy was pretty unsettled."

More recently, an employee named Chris "is positive she has seen the spirit. Chris was walking past some bulk bins of seeds and saw a person in a pink shirt kneeling down by one of the bins. Chris walked around the [2 metre] section of shelving and was about to offer her help when she realized that the 'customer' had vanished," Susan explained and added, "there is really no way someone could slip out of the store so quickly, or so quietly in the second it took Chris to go around that shelf. Also, the doors have bells [attached to them], which make quite a clatter. Chris was quite bothered. She knows she was not mistaken when she says she saw this person [and yet] the person was totally gone."

Chris was also the brunt of what might have been an attempt at a ghostly prank when she "had some papers pulled out of her hands. She knows that she just did not fumble and drop them. She could feel them being taken from her."

Susan also explained that a man who works there complains of someone (or something) bumping into him from time to time when no one visible is nearby.

In true ghostly fashion, this phantom has created "a very distinct" and localized area of inexplicably cold air. Two staff members walked back and forth "through a bitterly cold spot, just to reaffirm that they were both experiencing the same thing."

Susan concluded her anecdote with an interesting observation: "Most of the spirit's activities are around where the bulk seeds are kept. After the store was rearranged and the bulk bins moved, the spirit moved its activities too."

For whatever reason, this entity from another time or place is clearly attached to at least a portion of the here and now that makes up this haunted store.

Childish Illusion

After my book *More Ghost Stories of Alberta* was released in 1996, I began receiving fascinating tales of hauntings from all over the province. Although I had never given any thought to the possibility of a ghost in a daycare centre, one correspondent's experiences, as well as the photograph she sent me, convinced me that such a phenomenon does exist.

First, the staff at the daycare agreed they could sense a presence even when they knew they were alone. Next, those same workers began feeling as though someone was walking past and actually brushing up against them. They also began to detect unexplainable spots of cold air in random locations around the place—a classic sign of a ghostly presence.

It would seem from its antics that whatever haunts this daycare is a most benign spirit, likely the ghost of a child. The peaceful soul has probably been attracted to the fun of being around children and adults who are devoted to making those children happy. The resident spirit is credited with having pulled pranks that no one else could have. For instance, staff can occasionally hear their names being called, but when they respond, they are informed that no one had been calling them.

Once, during a weekend when the centre was closed, a maintenance worker was using a ladder as he made some repairs. He left the building and went out to his truck for a moment. By the time he came back to the room, his ladder had been moved a considerable distance. The poor man was badly unnerved because he knew for a fact that no other human being had been in, or even near, the building.

If walls could talk ... could they explain the origin of this sketchy spectre? (The children's faces have been obscured to protect their identities.)

One evening, long after the children and regular staff members had gone for the day, a member of the nighttime cleaning staff left several hours before she had intended to. She was cleaning a downstairs play area when she heard the sounds of footsteps running across the playroom directly above the room where she was working. Puzzled as to who might be responsible for making the noise, she used the intercom to contact her co-worker upstairs. When she was told that not only was no one running around up there but no noise at all was being made, she took a deep breath, calmed herself down and resumed her chores. It wasn't until the unmistakable sounds of little feet running on the floor above her started again that she left—in a hurry—and did not return until the next day when, once again, the place was alive with its usual joyful frenzy of child-related noises.

Adults aren't the only ones who have been aware of the ghostly presence. During a time that the children were sitting at tables eating their snacks, a little boy began waving enthusiastically at the window. When questioned about the gesture, he maintained that he was waving back at the child in the window who was waving to him. Although this particular toddler was known to be frightened of stories about even the most benign "monsters," he was decidedly pleased with the contact he'd made that day. No matter how she tried, the caregiver was not able to see the image that the child spoke of. She saw nothing in the window.

Such is apparently not always the case with the windows in that building. Sourceless shadows have been seen at the windows, especially during the children's naptime.

One summer, a special event was held at the daycare—a slumber party. The evening went extremely well and, as planned, staff took many snapshots of the children at their various activities. When the amateur photographers had the film from their cameras developed, they were in for a surprise. One of those photographs—one that they thought was simply a picture of three children enjoying themselves—included a child-like drawing on the wall, an outline of a little girl. There was no such image in the shot when the photo was taken, at least not one that the photographer had been able to see.

Signs of the haunting began to increase. The caregivers marvelled at toys that were heard, and seen, to move of their own accord. In an attempt to record this supernatural phenomenon, some of them brought a tape recorder into the centre one evening. When the cassette recording they made that night was replayed, the staff's suspicions seemed to be confirmed, for imprinted on the audio tape were the sounds of toys being played with when no one (visible) was anywhere in the building.

My correspondent is no longer working at the daycare, but she keeps in touch with her former colleagues. They have confirmed for her that the ghostly antics do continue, but the harmless spirit doesn't bother them.

The Apparition Wears Orange

Theatres are places where we invite both time and identity to shift. No wonder so many of them are haunted.

The following story is especially gratifying to me. Although I had heard about a theatre in Lethbridge, Alberta, that was reputed to be haunted, I had never been able to track down anyone who'd had a firsthand encounter with the ghost. I had virtually given up trying to get a detailed accounting of the tale when, much to my delight, just such a witness contacted me. This person had not only seen and felt the ghost in the theatre, but he was also a highly credible individual whose comments on the instances reflected a great deal of thought. Of all the ghost stories I've heard over the years, few have been told to me with such colour, obvious sincerity and vibrancy.

When Rod Blake (full name on file) initially contacted me through Lone Pine Publishing, he described himself as being "in the last year of completing a postgraduate degree at the University of Alberta." He also gave a thumbnail sketch of the paranormal experiences he'd had. I found the combination of the person and the events especially intriguing; we set up an appointment to meet at his office on the U of A campus.

When we met, Rod began the discussion by supplying some background, setting the stage for the story, so to speak. "From 1986 to 1991, I worked at the Lethbridge Centre Cinemas." For the first few months of his employment, Rod was an usher in the theatre. He worked in that capacity for "six months, maybe a little longer, maybe nine months. Then, I was promoted to doorman."

Although the ghost had been an acknowledged presence in the theatre for several years by that time, the haunting was not widely known, and Rod "knew nothing about the ghost story. This is important [to understand]," he stressed. "I had no prior knowledge."

The increased obligations associated with his promotion, however, were about to change that innocence. "One of the functions of the doorman was to close the theatre. The manager would leave about 45 minutes after the second movie started. Then everyone else [all the other employees] would leave, except for the doorman and the projectionist," Rod recalled.

"Generally, the movies would let out one before the other. They were timed that way. There was theatre Number One, a smaller theatre, and theatre Number Two, a little bit bigger. On this particular night, Number Two let out first so, when everyone left, I went in [and] checked it all out. I would walk down the aisles to make sure the back doors were closed, come [back] up and make sure everyone was out, and then close the doors."

After that initial check, there was little for Rod to do except "wait for the second theatre to let out." He continued, "I'd position myself, as I was supposed to, so that everyone would exit the building" rather than return to the lobby or anywhere else in the building.

Of course, there was the odd time that someone would need to use the washrooms or phones before leaving, but to do so, a person would have to pass the doorman, and Rod, like the other doormen, made a point of questioning any patron who was not leaving immediately. On this particular evening, Rod stated flatly, "I don't recall anyone walking past me."

Once the audiences had left the building, Rod's responsibilities included locking the building's front doors and then walking through all the areas of the theatre to make sure they were empty and secure.

"Then I did a general 'sweep' [walk-through] like always. I'd double check that the front doors were locked. I would go back and do another sweep—check the men's bathroom, the women's bathroom, including back into the theatre [that had most recently let out]," Rod detailed. At roughly this time each evening, the projectionist generally left, leaving Rod alone in the building to carry out his remaining responsibilities.

"What I had to do was shut off the lights in both theatres, then go into the projection room to [turn off] the lights there. It was my habit to look down [into the theatres]." One night, as Rod described it to me, "there was nothing in Number One, but, in theatre Number Two, there was a man in an orange coat sitting there. It wasn't a dull orange, but it wasn't a 'hunting orange' either. It was like a neon [colour], but brighter."

Having seen that there was someone left behind, Rod stopped his normal closing-up routine and made his way back downstairs into the auditorium. "That couldn't have taken more than a minute, guaranteed. I went into theatre Number One and no one's there, but I'm feeling a sense of eeriness. I'm sensing an eeriness and I'm feeling uncomfortable. I'm not generally a fearful person but I felt absolutely fearful."

In addition to the raw fear, Rod felt "a sense of time being altered maybe a little bit."

Despite his extreme unease, Rod's dedication to his job demanded that he run through the entire closing-up procedure once again. "I did another sweep, checked the whole thing out again. I went back upstairs to shut the lights off, looked down [into the theatres] again. There was no one there."

This visual affirmation that he was alone did not shake Rod's feelings of discomfort and concern. He very much wanted to leave the theatre where he'd seen (and then not seen!) the strange presence but thought that to do so without any follow-up would be irresponsible.

"I figured the safe thing to do was to leave a note for [the theatre manager]. I wrote him a note saying, 'I saw this person in the theatre after I closed up. He had an orange coat on, so I checked again but no one was here.'"

Feeling that there was little else he could accomplish by staying in the theatre—a place he very much wanted to leave—the unnerved young man headed home. The next time he was at work, however, his boss made a point of speaking to Rod about his unusual experience.

"He talked to me about it between movies. He asked me about [the encounter], then, he told me about the ghost."

As the resident spirit in the theatre is thought to be that of a man who was a well-known Lethbridge resident, Rod suggested that we refer to the ghost as "Frederick." In life, Frederick was closely associated with the theatres.

But how, I wondered, was Rod's boss so sure that the image he had seen that night had been that of Frederick? The answer was simple and quite convincing. Apparently, in life, the man always wore an orange coat.

Rod continued, "That's the part that really made me think, because I'd had no prior knowledge. If I'd had prior knowledge that there was potentially anything to do with a ghost or an orange coat, then I could see my mind playing tricks on me ..." The man then let his thought trail off unfinished.

That sighting was not the only time the ghost of the long-dead man made himself known to Rod. The next incident "happened about a year after the first one, so I'd found out the stories about Frederick. I always kept my eyes open and I never felt the same [at work] after the first experience [although] I'd been told that [the ghost] was supposedly very helpful and there to protect the theatre. He wasn't there to cause problems."

Despite having heard these reassuring words, Rod was frightened one more time by the phantom. "The second incident was a lot more brief and a lot scarier."

Again, Rod was alone in the theatre, closing up after

the second show. He described the frightening experience as follows:

> I was going up the steps to shut off the lights. They were metal steps I was going up and as I'm going up I'm hearing someone coming down the steps. The sounds of the footsteps are clear. The metal steps are open. You can look through them. There are big spaces between the steps. I stopped dead. I looked up. There was absolutely no one, but the sound was coming down and I could follow the movement of the sound down the steps. This really scared me. I felt instant fear. I followed [the footfalls] about four or five steps as they came down. I turned around and ran out the back door and didn't even double check that it was locked. I knew the doors were locked but I also knew the lights were on because I hadn't made it up there [to turn them off]. I thought about the pros and cons and I thought, *What's it going to hurt if the theatre lights are on? It's going to burn a little extra electricity, that's all.*

Rod shrugged off his conscience about the wasted resources: "I thought to myself, *I'm not going back in there.* That was intense fear. I felt very, very scared. I drove home and the next day at work, right off the mark, I told my boss [what had happened]."

If Rod hadn't been such an honest and forthright employee, the theatre manager would probably never have suspected anything unusual had occurred, for when the theatre was first opened the following morning, all was as it should have been. The doors were locked and the lights were off. Apparently, Frederick's ghost had secured the building for the night. It was the least he could do after having scared away the person who was supposed to perform those chores.

And Rod is certainly not the only one to have had encounters with the resident spectre. "The stories that were told about Frederick were told very seriously and, past that, we just didn't talk about it. I didn't push it. It was just part of the culture there. I still to this day really believe that Frederick walks in that theatre. I'm absolutely convinced that he was there. Someone was there. Someone was watching me."

Another theatre in Lethbridge is also rumoured to have a ghost. According to one of a series of articles written by Virgil Grandfield and published by the *Lethbridge Herald* in October 1999, the Genevieve E. Yates Memorial Theatre is haunted.

On one occasion an employee named Dawn first heard and then saw a group of little girls playing "Ring Around the Rosy." As Dawn approached the children they looked at her before running into the next room. Dawn immediately turned on the lights in that room but there was nothing there. The playful singing images simply vanished.

Another employee, Linda, was vacuuming the auditorium early one morning. Over the noise of the vacuum cleaner she heard female singing voices. She quickly shut the machine off and began to check through the theatre to find the choir. Although the beautiful choral music continued for almost a minute, Linda's search confirmed that, just as she thought, she was the only (live) person in the building.

Where are They Now?

Edmonton's Rialto Theatre was demolished in 1987, that much is known. We cannot be as sure of what happened to the ghosts who had long haunted the place. According to a 1996 Halloween article in the *Edmonton Journal*, the downtown movie house was the permanent home to the ghosts of three people—a former projectionist, a woman who had been murdered and a child who had tragically been trampled to death.

Phantoms of the Pumphouse

The general manager of Calgary's Pumphouse Theatres, Leslie Holth, explained that while only one of the ghost stories from the theatres had ever been published, many others have been "passed from ear to ear over the past 30 years."

Considering the building's history, it's not much of a surprise that it has collected its share of resident spirits. Built in 1913 as Pumphouse #2, the place was a maze of pipes that drew water from the adjacent Bow River to supply the needs of Calgarians. Rumour had it that at least one worker died in the building during those early years. Tenacious research, however, has failed to come up with any confirmation of that story. In the mid-1920s, the Elbow River became the city's water source and old #2 was no longer required. But, the building was not demolished.

"A lot of those pipes are still there, under the river, and a third of the building is the original structure," Leslie told me.

Inevitably, over the years, the building deteriorated. When the Great Depression cut its swath across the Prairies, the solid structure with its proximity to the railway tracks became adequate, if unofficial, temporary accommodation for the hoboes riding the rails in search of a better place than what they'd left.

Although we'd all like to believe that everyone who suffered through the Depression was a paragon of virtue merely down on his or her luck, such was not the case. The vagrants did not have much in the way of possessions and some had

The ghosts in this theatre may date back to when the building really was a pumphouse.

even less respect for life. Their system of justice tended not to involve formal sources. As a result, many thefts, fights, fatal accidents and even murders often went unnoticed and certainly unreported. Most people who accept that the Pumphouse theatre facility is haunted believe any ghosts hail from that era and those circumstances.

By the late 1960s the building had outlived its usefulness and was scheduled to be torn down. By coincidence, about that time, drama teacher and theatre lover Joyce Doolittle "discovered" the site. She led an enthusiastic group of workers, and by 1972 the venue staged its first live production. Since then, the operation has flourished and become a multi-stage theatre facility, collectively known as The Pumphouse Theatres.

All of this theatrical success has perhaps been somewhat amusing to the theatre's long-standing ethereal residents. In 1979, then-manager Bob Eberle stated, "We may have a new theatre but the ghosts of the past still haunt us."

That statement is apparently still true today. Leslie Holth explained that "during a performance in the Joyce Doolittle Theatre (the 88-year-old side of the facility), the director was sitting in the audience when the house lights went to black. In the seconds before the stage lights went up, music was heard over the loud speakers." Leslie explained that normally this would not be a problem, but the director had specifically indicated that music not be played at the beginning of the performance. During intermission, the director stormed into the control booth demanding to know who had decided to add music to her show at the last minute. As Leslie noted, "Both the sound operator and the stage manager were dumbfounded. They hadn't turned on any music and, in fact, were equally confused by the mysterious [musical] presence."

That incident, along with the following one, might indicate that at least one of the manifestations in the Pumphouse is (or was) a music lover. According to the theatre's website, the "wife of one of the employees was in the Joyce Doolittle Theatre lobby and heard ... what sounded like a music box playing in the corner. She called her husband and asked if any music was being played in the dressing room or the theatre. He told her 'No' and inquired as to why [she would ask]."

The woman explained that she had clearly heard such distinct sounds. The employee was dumbfounded. His wife would have had no idea that a player piano used to sit in the area where she heard the music. The enigma was never solved.

Leslie Holth adds, "Over the years several employees and theatre volunteers have noted the occasional 'visitation.' Sudden cold; hairs rising on the back of your neck; sounds coming from the darkened theatre, the sounds of footsteps and laughter have all been reported or experienced. Although many people dismiss the possibility, there are those of us who verbally greet the building's 'residents' upon opening the doors each morning. Who knows? I'd rather be safe than sorry."

Leslie explained her philosophy of respect and acceptance: "They say we should befriend that which we don't know and thereby will come to appreciate a greater understanding of our world." With such human compassion in those governing their haunted area, what ghost would ever want to leave Pumphouse #2?

Chapter 5

Spirit's Inn

Some businesses, such as inns and restaurants,

can provide temporary substitutes for our homes.

Perhaps this is why they are frequently also

home to ghosts.

Business Assurance

Many months before I knew I would be writing this book, my friends Jan and Rose Jones invited me to be their guest for lunch at a quaint tea house near Ardrossan. I had already accepted the kind invitation when Jan added the kicker—"It's haunted, by a very protective spirit."

Sunny Alberta was showing off its best the day the three of us drove out for our planned luncheon. Marlhine, the owner of the Treasure Chest and Antiques Limited, greeted us with sincerity as well as justifiable pride in the unique restaurant she has created.

Lunch was delicious, and the conversation most intriguing, for Jan Jones has an unusual and interesting hobby. With her digital camera, Jan has found that she can capture anomalies—orbs, usually—in photographs. Many people believe that these orbs, invisible to the naked eye, indicate the presence of a paranormal being—possibly a ghost. (I became one of those "many" after Jan showed me a series of pictures she had taken in which an orb followed us down a staircase and through the halls of a building we were touring—a building that is known to be haunted!)

On the day of our luncheon, Jan brought her camera with her. She had been at the Treasure Chest and Antiques Limited several times before and, after listening to Marlhine's matter-of-fact explanation about their resident spirit, Jan had successfully captured enough shots of orbs that she was able to give Marlhine a photo album full of such snapshots. The ghost-hunting expedition that day was just as rewarding and, as this was my first experience with such photography, an exciting time for me.

Before I had the opportunity to call Marlhine to ask her more about her interesting ghostly anecdotes, she sent me a note indicating she'd be willing to share the story of her haunted tea house with me for my book. And this she did, during a lengthy and most enjoyable telephone conversation early in the year 2001.

Marlhine began by explaining that 15 years ago, she had planned to operate a gift shop in Ardrossan, and so she opened the Treasure Chest. "I installed two wood cookstoves, one on the top storey and one on the bottom. They were for heat originally, but then I began putting on coffee for the customers. Pretty soon after that, I started to bake muffins and not long after that people started saying to me, 'Why don't you make a stew on a Sunday?'"

While Marlhine appreciated people's enthusiasm, she realized that the food part of the business "was going to take over my Treasure Chest." She began thinking about all the implications of that possibility.

"I kept thinking about it, picturing it. If I could only find my dream home and then move it out here, then I would have a restaurant, or a tea house or something, I didn't even know what to call it," Marlhine recalled.

There was clearly no sense of urgency in the shop owner's mind: "I wasn't going to say I want it next year or the year after—just 'if ever.' I eventually told three people, two of them were actually scroungers, so I knew that if anyone ever ran into the dream house, they would. I kind of drew out what I had in mind—I'm a terrible drawer but it was a two-storey house with siding and pillars on the veranda. It had hardwood floors and a tub on legs. There

A good-natured ghost named Harry cheerfully announces his arrival when he visits this tea house.

was an archway between the living room and dining room. Just everything (in that sketch) would be my dream."

Marlhine continued, "Five days later, one of [the scroungers] phoned me. He said, 'Did you see that place they're going to demolish in Vegreville? I think you'd better get down there because I think it's going [to be torn down] next week.'"

Her curiosity sparked, Marlhine lost no time in making the drive to the nearby community. When she arrived she could hardly believe her eyes, for there, "in a state of disrepair," was her dream home—the house she had sketched.

"It was exactly as I drew it; I don't mean *almost*," she emphasized before describing the house. "The front door was oak and the windows were all the original single diamond [style]. There was no hesitation on my part. I just told them it was mine, and I built a basement and had it pulled out here."

After many hours of work, the old place was ready to open for business as a tea house. "The day before we opened, we were making some soups and a batch of bread in the kitchen. All of a sudden we all heard a male voice call out, 'I'm home.' I went to the front door. I knew it was locked but I thought maybe it was the kind of door that didn't lock properly. There was nobody there. Then the staff all came out because they said they'd definitely heard someone."

Despite everyone's conviction about what they'd heard, there was no one except themselves in the house, and the front door was still as securely locked as it had been immediately after they'd all gone in hours before. Although they were all puzzled, Marlhine explained, "Nobody was really scared and we just let it go."

It's just as well no one *was* frightened by the sound of the disembodied voice calling out a greeting, for the phantom voice was regularly heard in the transported and converted house.

"It would happen so often, a man's voice calling 'I'm home,' but no one was there."

Perhaps feeling that he was no longer drawing enough attention to himself just by coming 'home,' the ghost began to play little tricks. For instance, Marlhine remembered, "One day a wooden spoon flew off the table. Two of us saw it. It just flew off the table and on to the floor. It was always just little things like that."

As is often the case with a place that is haunted by one particular spirit, the people associated with the tea house gave their revenant a name. "We started calling him Harry. Whenever anything happened we'd say, 'Oh well, it's just Harry.' It always kind of thrilled us."

Word of Marlhine's successful business in the renovated house spread until the home's original owners, by then residents of an island in British Columbia, heard about it. Curious to see how their old family home looked after all these years, they made a point of visiting.

"While they were here," Marlhine recalled, "I was asking them questions about who lived in the house. Then one of the waitresses said to them, 'And did Harry live here too?'"

The visitors seemed a bit surprised by the question but simply explained that no one named Harry had lived in the house although they'd had an uncle by that name. Then it was the guests' turn to ask a question. "How do you know Harry?" they inquired.

Marlhine chuckled as she relayed the conversation that had ensued: "We told them the stories and they roared with laughter. Their Uncle Harry had always come in through the front door and he had always hollered, 'I'm home' as he came in. That was always his greeting. They said he loved it here."

The family also confirmed that Harry had been the sort of person who loved to play tricks on people. "So that's why the wooden spoon went flying."

I pointed out to Marlhine that it was an amazing coincidence that of all the names available to her she'd chosen to call her resident phantom by the name that actually had been his in life.

"You do wonder how that ever happened," she replied with a tone of puzzlement.

Marlhine also wonders if Harry's presence had anything to do with an amazing coincidence that occurred at the tea house once. "We found a picture in one of the walls [during the renovation process]. It was a picture of a woman. I put it in a photo album with a note asking 'Does anyone know this beautiful woman?' About a year after that, two women from Vegreville were sitting here and they were looking at the album. One said to the other, 'Well, look, that's you,' and it was her. Fifty years prior she was a house-cleaner in this home and someone had taken her photograph. Somehow it had ended up between the walls of the house. Then there she was—50 years later—sitting here looking at it."

To this day, Marlhine wonders if that "coincidence" was somehow orchestrated by Harry's ghostly hand.

Marlhine concluded our conversation in a delightfully understated fashion. "Nothing earth shattering has happened here but, over the years, ever since I've had this wonderful home, people have said to me, 'Aren't you scared to leave [artifacts and ornaments] out like you do?' And I've always said, 'No,' something seems to be protecting this place."

At a time when theft has become a real and expensive problem for many business owners, Marlhine's enterprise has remained untouched by crime. "Really, it's just been amazing. There are [valuable decorative pieces] in bathrooms, out in the yard. We are protected, I know that."

Maybe there should be special insurance rates for such a special place that is so effectively, and permanently, protected.

Where History Lives—Literally

The highway sign pointing to Nanton quotes the town's slogan, "Where History Lives." Those words might be truer than anyone had intended, for here, some 25 kilometres south of High River, Alberta, at least one former resident may still be roaming about the second floor of the Auditorium Hotel. If he is, he may feel he is in something of a time-warp because like Lacombe and several other towns in Alberta, the downtown of Nanton has been refurbished to resemble the town as it stood in 1913. The ghost, however, is probably a much more recent anomaly—likely the soul of Rex Irwin, a regular and well-liked hotel patron who died in his hotel room some 50 years ago.

Free Room and Phantom

Nearly every small town has one—a local watering hole. Usually it's a bar in a hotel, and usually the bar does more business than the hotel. This is certainly true of the hotel in a town 50 kilometres northeast of Edmonton.

Over the years, I would occasionally hear rumours about this particular hotel being haunted, but it wasn't until Gerry West wrote to me that I finally had a firsthand account of the ghost and his activities. Gerry's encounters came about when he took a friend up on an offer of free lodging at the hotel.

Gerry explained that he "had moved back to town in September of 1993." He had recently completed college and his finances were limited, so when a friend offered him a free room in the hotel, Gerry readily agreed and took over the biggest of the eight rooms on the second floor. All went well until the ghost, probably a former tenant of that room, made his presence known.

"One night in late October, I heard footsteps walking around outside my room, so I got up to look around," Gerry began. "I looked in all the rooms upstairs and went down to the bar. I couldn't find anyone so I went back to my room, turned out the lights and went back to bed. I had just lain down when the window shade snapped straight out from the window at a 90-degree angle."

Concerned, Gerry once more got out of bed, this time to make sure that the window was closed. "When I checked the window I found that it had been painted shut and could not be opened."

To make the situation even more distressing, Gerry could smell the unmistakable odour of fresh cigar smoke in his room. Despite the bizarre circumstances, Gerry stayed in the room until morning when he paid a visit to his parents' home.

"Over coffee, I told my Mom and Dad the story of the night's events. My Dad told me that many years ago, there was an old druggist who stayed in that room. Dad said he was a grumpy old man who looked like Winston Churchill and that he always smoked cigars."

Then Gerry's father added the clincher: the "grumpy old man" died in the room Gerry was staying in. Gerry's mother, who at one time had worked daytime shifts in the hotel, was able to confirm that the ghost was not active only at night. "One afternoon she watched as a pool ball rolled across the pool table by itself. She noticed the smell of cigar smoke when this occurred."

And the Wests are certainly not the only people to have been made aware of the phantom's existence. Fortunately, he's not a nasty spirit, merely mischievous. He once startled a woman working in the hotel when she tried to use the washroom. If she closed the door and locked it, the ghost would simply unlock and open it. Conversely, if she left the door open, he would close it.

Like most ghosts, this one loved to play with electrical appliances, turning them on and off at random and adjusting the volume on the jukebox to *his* liking. The resident spirit is also generally blamed when alarm clocks set by the hotel's guests either ring at the wrong time or not at all. Perhaps in his ghostly realm, time is not as important as it is to us human beings.

"It's No Secret"

I have had wonderfully warm receptions from people when I've asked if I may retell their ghost story in one of my books. Even though I am used to such reactions, I was surprised by the warmth and enthusiasm of Darlene, co-owner of the haunted Honey Pot restaurant in Wainwright, a town near the eastern border of Alberta.

"I'd be honoured," was her reply, "it's no secret in Wainwright that we're haunted. We call our ghost 'Charlie.' We say 'Good night' to him when we leave and 'Good morning' when we come in."

Darlene's husband has lived on the property all his life. "He certainly believes there's a presence here but has never encountered anything. I seem to be the person Charlie's directing himself toward. That's fine, I guess, I'm open to it. He likes me."

I was curious as to when Darlene became aware of the ghost, especially as she had described herself as a former skeptic. "Right away," was her immediate reply. "I was not sensitive to this sort of thing before I became involved with this particular building. I wasn't a believer."

The incident that caused the 180-degree shift in Darlene's belief system happened over 20 years ago, when she and her husband were newly married and living in the apartment above the store. "I saw a figure one evening. As soon as I looked back, it was gone."

With only that brief introduction, Charlie's attempts to attract Darlene's attention were on.

"I was alone in the building," Darlene began. She was standing near the ice machine, which has a cover on it and is kept closed. Inexplicably, "from the periphery of my vision I could see an ice cube coming directly at me. I turned to look at it and as soon as I did, the ice cube dropped directly to the floor by my foot."

Knowing she was alone in the building, Darlene nevertheless began to look for something that might have propelled the ice cube. There was nothing—nothing that she could see, anyway.

Another time Darlene felt a pressure on her shoulder. I asked her if it felt warm or cold or if it felt like a hand. "I don't know," she acknowledged simply. "I was so startled by it that I fell. I didn't allow myself time to figure it out."

Despite occasional occurrences that have rattled Darlene's composure, overall she declares that she is not frightened. "We have been in business for 23 years in a small town, which isn't easy. I'm sure that if there are spirits then they are capable of a lot and if this one had wanted to, he could have done a lot. He hasn't."

The general belief is actually that Charlie's presence is good for business. "We're usually really busy when we feel his presence. We find that if somebody's heard him cough, then that day we'll be busy. If we haven't felt him for a while then we're slow."

Charlie certainly is an interesting character. "He has quite a striking personality," Darlene attests. Twice now when she's closed up the restaurant at night and then reopened it in the morning she's found damaged cutlery and glasses at one particular table. "There hadn't been a break-in," Darlene assured me. She thinks that Charlie, having a special fondness for her, was lonely and angry when she left him alone on those nights.

Darlene compared her resident wraith to a child who likes attention but won't show off when you want him to. "We have people coming in the [restaurant] wanting to meet Charlie but he'll never do anything at those times. It's like he's behind your back laughing at you."

He can also be mischievous. "One time I was walking with someone. I had walked past a hallway and when I came back, a chair had been moved in front of my path as if to stop me. It seemed very purposeful, like the instance with the ice cube did. I've also felt him brush by me."

Darlene continued, "A cook and I were standing in the kitchen. There was a pot on the stove. There was nothing in it and the stove wasn't on, but the pot flew 6 feet [2 metres] in between us. It didn't travel fast as if someone had knocked it. It was quite slow, as if someone were carrying it. It wasn't as if someone had thrown it."

Other tenants of the apartment above the restaurant have been aware of the ghost's presence in the residence, just as Darlene and her husband were when they lived there. Three gentlemen who rented the place one summer were all convinced it was haunted, but they thought the ghost was a female. "Perhaps she's Charlotte, then," Darlene quipped.

The experience of another tenant, Tara, might bear that theory out as well. Despite the strange looks she'd received from friends when she rented a place that was accepted as being haunted, the young woman settled into the apartment and into a comfortable routine. "When I came home from work each day I laid my purse, keys and sunglasses on a small table inside the doorway. One morning as I was leaving for work, none of those items could be found. I'm always very careful to lock my door as soon as I get in and no one else was living in the building at that time. Luckily, I had a spare set of keys."

Without her purse or sunglasses, Tara headed out for the day. "That evening (it was summer and so still light out), I saw something shining on the railing about 10 feet [3 metres] from my door—my keys and sunglasses. My purse was sitting on the little table where I usually left it."

It would seem that Charlie, or Charlotte, had been up to mischief again!

There are several theories as to who the ghost may have been when he walked this plane. Darlene explained, "The man who originally built the place was murdered." That crime has never been solved, so the ghost could be the unsettled soul of the victim.

Another theory has it that the building was once used as a brothel and a gambling den which catered to railway workers and the military base. Rumour has it that during that time one man was shot and another hanged himself.

"Who knows?" Darlene asks rhetorically. "It could have been someone we served. I have to say, though, he has to be of a good nature."

Although Darlene thoroughly enjoys the phantom's presence, she did explain that they've "been trying to tell him to go. We tell him to go where it's peaceful because he's been around forever. He's been wandering for a long time as a lost soul."

Dancing in Their Own Time

As documented in my previous book *More Ghost Stories of Alberta*, Calgary's Cross House restaurant not only is a terrific place for a relaxing meal but is also haunted. The house is named for A.E. Cross, one of the men who founded the world-renowned Calgary Stampede. The spirit of Mrs. Cross, wife of A.E., is still occasionally present in her former home although she's been dead for years. Even the long-deceased Mr. Cross has made his presence known. Many years after his death, he has been driven, by cab, to the place that was his home.

When my daughter and I had lunch at the Cross House in December 2000, we were fascinated to hear George Diament, the manager, tell us that suspiciously paranormal happenings have continued to occur in this delightfully haunted house-cum-restaurant.

George began, "I remember an instance where a young woman was carrying a tray from the kitchen out to the rooms where the guests had congregated. She was an experienced server who'd proved herself to us as a great asset. This one day, however, just as she walked into the room where the guests were, she 'dropped' the tray."

George was surprised that such an experienced and usually reliable worker would have such an accident—not nearly as surprised, though, as was the woman it happened to. Despite everyone's shock and embarrassment, they cleaned up the "accident" as quickly and thoroughly as they could in order not to further disrupt the social occasion.

It wasn't until closing that the employee came to speak to her boss. George told me, "She insisted that she hadn't merely dropped the tray, that it hadn't overbalanced in any way. She knew how to carry such heavy, precarious loads without incident. She insisted that something or someone (unseen) had knocked at the tray from underneath—hard enough to send the tray and all its contents flying."

Why this should have happened is anyone's guess. All that's known for sure is that an experienced server was performing a normal function when an extremely abnormal—or should we say paranormal—event occurred. No explanation has ever been found for the strange occurrence, but the server is as convinced today as she was then that the "accident" was caused when an unseen force punched, or pushed, the bottom of the platter she'd been comfortably and safely carrying.

Recently a wedding reception was held at the Cross House. Of course, as with most weddings, many photographs were taken of the festivities. When the couple returned from their honeymoon they were eager to invite their friends over to look through all the pictures from their special day.

Most of the shots were fine, some were spectacular, but a few were not. Those few were nothing short of puzzling, for on a roll of film devoted strictly to that wedding reception, a few pictures showed an indistinct image of one particular couple dancing among the other celebrants on the dance floor.

Initially the amateur photographer was annoyed that his camera had not photographed this one couple as well as it had all the others. The more the pictures were passed

The ghost at the Cross House has apparently attracted other spirits.

around and examined by those who had been at the reception, the more puzzling the enigma became, because no one—not one person who'd attended that small wedding party—recognized the couple. In fact, no one had ever even seen the pair before.

The conclusion was finally reached that these hazy dancers who were so clearly enjoying themselves were not wedding guests at all. They were ghosts, ghosts who had slipped into the Cross House, no doubt drawn by the joyful celebration and the rare opportunity for a waltz in *their* time.

Fast Food Phantom

I had long heard rumours that a fast food outlet on Edmonton's Argyll Road was haunted. It was only recently, however, that I was fortunate enough to learn about the ghost from someone who'd had several supernatural experiences while working in the restaurant.

Collin began by explaining that in the late 1970s he was employed at the haunted restaurant. He usually worked nights and was in charge of the closing procedures. "Ideally, the shift should have run from 4 PM to midnight," he began. Unfortunately, with the number of duties necessary in the closing process, it could be hours later than that before Collin was able to leave.

This meant that Collin spent a lot of time alone in the basement office of the restaurant with only maintenance people working for a few hours on the main floor.

"In the basement was the regional head office, our training room, our office, the stockroom which was a caged, locked stockroom, lockers for the staff, washrooms and change rooms and a little lunch room." That was the era of pinball machines, and the restaurant supplied one in the lunch room for their youthful staff to play during their breaks. "The lunch room was connected [to the main floor] by an intercom system, so if you did get busy upstairs you could always call somebody up off their break. Many times, particularly in the evening when I knew everybody was up on the floor and the office staff had gone home for the evening, if the intercom was on you would hear things like the pinball machine playing.

Not just the usual ping-ping noise that those machines made every now and then, but it sounded as if someone was playing it."

Unfailingly, Collin went downstairs to see who was playing the game but "there was no one there." In addition, "lights would flash on and off occasionally for no apparent reason."

Those who acknowledged the ghost generally felt she was female. Collin explained that when he was working in his out-of-the-way office he "could smell fresh perfume around me. This could be at 1 AM and the last female was gone by 11:30 PM. It felt like you had somebody watching you, looking over your shoulder."

Collin added that those sensations caused "the hair on the back of my neck to stand up."

Collin explained that a maintenance worker had an even closer encounter with the spirit. "He went down into the stockroom, which is a locked cage, to pick up some cleaning supplies. He unlocks it, picks up his stuff, turns around, locks the cage up again and says 'Hello' to the person standing there watching him ... this blonde lady in her mid-20s, she was standing inside the locked cage. He looked away for a second, looked back and she was gone."

Eventually Collin was transferred to another location but one evening was back at his old "haunt" to pick up his girlfriend after her shift. It seemed that some of the staff from another store had been sent for a few hours that evening to work at the haunted restaurant.

Collin recalled, "These guys were in pure panic. They said the lights in the basement were going on and off, the pinball machine was going nuts, they were just panic-stricken. The ghost must have been showing off."

As far as Collin knows, no one has ever investigated who the ghost might be. Most people involved in this haunting, it seems, prefer to deal with this ghost by ignoring or denying it, and for good reason, for Collin concluded, "It was an uncomfortable, uneasy feeling when she was around."

Whether or not the presence is still in the building is unknown, for at this writing, the restaurant is closed and the building is boarded up.

Chapter 6

Alberta Anomalies

Some paranormal stories refuse to be neatly categorized,

but that doesn't mean they are not tantalizing.

The following are a few examples of such tales.

Sightings

In January 1998, a spectacular early-morning blaze seriously damaged the old Lorraine Apartments on 12th Avenue in Calgary's southwest quadrant. The beautiful old brick building had been a city landmark since its construction in 1914, but after the fire the gutted building bore little resemblance to the stately structure it once was.

The destruction of the apartment building was a great loss, not only because our young province has relatively few stately and historic buildings but also because this particular building had always been interesting to anyone with a love for local ghost lore. One Halloween in the mid-1990s, Patricia called a radio phone-in show to relate an experience she and her husband had while living in the Lorraine. One evening, as the two were relaxing in their suite, they heard the sound of someone knocking at their window. Startled, they both jumped to their feet and bolted to the window. There, staring back at them, was a man. The image was clear and real enough that they could even identify the type of hat he was wearing. Unfortunately, that clarity did nothing to calm the startled couple, for they knew that the vision they were staring at could not possibly be real. This window was well above ground level and there were no exterior ledges on which a person could perch.

Furthermore, Patricia and her husband realized that it wasn't a man looking in at them but merely a man's head. The disembodied head, topped with a fedora, disappeared as mysteriously as it had appeared.

Today, if that poor soul returned to the Lorraine he would have nothing to look through. The burned-out shell remains, at the time of this writing, boarded up—both literally with plywood and figuratively with the red tape that ensued because the building was being sold when the fire occurred. Fortunately, there is still hope that the building will one day be repaired and refurbished to its status of landmark.

One of the oldest and most charming of the residential sections of St. Albert is Grandin. On Greenwich Crescent in Grandin, people report seeing a vision—a ghostly vision of a girl, estimated to be in her early teens.

The child's apparition wanders along the street aimlessly, usually at twilight. People are able to describe her as having long, flowing blonde hair. Despite this detail, no investigations have been able to determine who the girl might have been when she was alive or why she haunts the area.

The Galt Museum in Lethbridge is well known for being haunted by the ghost of George Bailey, who died in a particularly gruesome accident there in the 1930s when the building was a hospital, but apparently Bailey is not the only ghost there. According to an article written by Virgil Grandfield for the *Lethbridge Herald*, at least one person, Louis Soop, has seen the ghostly images of two little boys staring out of second-floor windows.

When he saw the images, Soop had just left the museum and knew for a fact that the building was empty. He also knew that the windows where he saw the images were so high off the floor that a real child would barely be able to peek out. Despite this physical fact, Soop had clearly seen the lads' torsos and heads.

In discussing the images Soop had seen, Grandfield noted that many little boys had been treated in the Sunbeam Children's Ward when the building served as the area's hospital.

In the northwest of our province, a legendary phantom walks near, or on, the Dunvegan Bridge. The setting of this tale would be dramatic even if it didn't include a ghost, for anyone approaching the valley of the mighty Peace River from the north travels down a long winding hill. It is just at this point that the ghost of a nun appears. She glides effortlessly, "almost airborne," according to the reports of some witnesses.

She appears so real that people have stopped to offer her assistance but their entreaties apparently go unheard. The image simply continues along on her ghostly route before vanishing. Conversely, when people go out in search of the strange spirit, she tends to be more aware of human beings and actually seems to "spy" on those who've come to "spy" on her. Her clothing is said to be easily visible—almost luminous.

In the late 1890s, the Sisters of Providence operated a boarding school at the St. Augustine Mission in Dunvegan. Many epidemics swept through the area in those early days and it is theorized that the enduring spirit may be the ghost of one of those killed at that time.

The ghost is so much a part of the local folklore that a painting of her image hangs in the town's art gallery. Artist Bob Guest created the work from memory, for he has seen the apparition on several occasions dating back to the 1970s.

Another female apparition has been seen on the shores of hauntingly beautiful Lake Agnes in the Rocky Mountains. Your best bet to see this ghost is to hike the 8 kilometres from Lake Louise to this lake, which is at an elevation of over 2000 metres. The manifestation is said to frequent the shores and occasionally approach the quaint European-style tea house situated nearby. Even if you don't catch a glimpse of the paranormal image, you will be treated to some of the world's most spectacular scenery.

In the delightfully named community of Springbrook, just south of Red Deer, there is said to be the transparent image of an old woman who wanders the streets at night. The community, my informant advised, "used to be an army base, but now has been converted to private housing." Perhaps the poor lost soul is still waiting for an enlisted relative to come home from a mission.

In 1982, journalist Cristine Bye of the *Calgary Herald* reported that an elderly man wearing old-fashioned clothing introduced himself to two men who had been walking through Calgary's Riley Park.

"I'm Ezra Riley," the image maintained before giving the men his life's history, including the fact that he had donated the land for the park bearing his name—at the time of his death some 70 years previously.

The news article concluded with a description the witnesses gave of watching the oddly dressed, seemingly out-of-place man, walk away—before simply vanishing.

According to James Martin's book *Secrets of the City*, Guy Weadick, one of the founders of the world-famous Calgary Stampede, still roams the Stampede Grounds. Not too unusual you may think—except that Weadick died in 1952.

Casper, the Mischievous Ghost

Ghost stories, by their very nature, are enigmatic. (Perhaps mortals are equally puzzling to those in the spirit world!) Sarah and Jack's ghost story, however, is even more curious than most.

The Red Deer couple (whose correct and full names are on file) were well into middle age when they first began to notice the presence they came to call "Casper." Jack and Sarah's encounters strongly indicate that their ghostly companion is a poltergeist. Although one can certainly experience a haunting at any age, poltergeists are more commonly associated with young people, most often teenagers. Casper's timing may have been off in that regard but, in true poltergeist fashion, his staying power has been nothing short of amazing.

Sarah began, "For the last 30 or 35 years, we have, at different times, felt the presence of someone or something who seems to enjoy taking or borrowing things."

As the items that disappear are not of any serious consequence, the couple has assumed that the spectre is friendly and therefore have named their invisible thief "Casper," after the old comic strip "Casper, the Friendly Ghost."

Often a spirit in a house can be traced back to a former occupant, but Sarah and Jack's situation could not be that easily explained. "This was a new house. We were the first to live in it. Or, did Casper move in first?" Sarah wondered.

As with most new houses, the basement, one of Casper's favourite haunts, was still unfinished. This meant that the "studs and floor joists were all open. The stairs went down from the landing at the back door (which was always kept locked). Jack stored his old two-foot, wooden level up in the beam at the foot of the stairs. It was very noticeable as you started downstairs," Sarah explained. "One day it was missing."

While the strange disappearance must have been something of a shock, its reappearance was an even bigger shock. "The level showed up in exactly the place it had gone missing from—a year and a half later." Presumably, by that time, Casper no longer needed the tool.

Although Casper's games may have been intermittent, his presence, Sarah felt, was close to constant. He even became something of a companion for the woman. "I never felt alone but it wasn't scary, just rather peaceful that I was not alone, as we were away from most of our family and didn't have many friends calling by. When I was vacuuming or working alone around the house, I would look behind me expecting to see someone." Sarah's eyes, however, never confirmed what she had "felt."

Sarah may have thought Casper's company was a plus, but his games could make it difficult for her to accomplish chores, especially mending. "Casper seemed to like annoying me by taking my darning needles. I could be sitting sewing when my big darning needle would just be gone out of my hand. I would stand up to search, expecting to find it in my lap or chair but it was never there. We would even turn the chair over but never found anything. I must have lost three or four needles that way at different times. One day while we were doing extra cleaning, Jack was dusting the top of an inside door frame and he pushed off one of the needles that had been missing."

Casper's pranks were sometimes more difficult to deal with. Sarah remembered being short-tempered at "a time when suddenly my needle was missing. I spoke out loud without thinking, 'That's enough of this. Stop it.' But, sometime later, feeling bad about my harsh words and thinking that Casper might have left, I said, 'I'm sorry. I really didn't mean it.'"

Eventually Jack and Sarah moved from that house to another new one. They didn't have to wait long to find out if their long-time invisible roommate followed. "Casper was busier than ever. Many times things would be missing, but whatever it was would usually turn up later in its original place."

Casper's behaviour up to this point had already indicated that he was a poltergeist, but his trip with Jack and Sarah to the Philippines removed all doubt. Poltergeists are always associated with people rather than places, and they have been known to travel across continents and oceans to be with the humans they have chosen to haunt. This is exactly what Casper did.

"We were with a tour group arriving in Manila in the morning, after flying all night. We were assigned our rooms [and planned] to rest before travelling on. We got our key and went to our room. Going inside, the first thing I saw was an earring on the floor just a few feet inside the door. As it looked familiar, I picked it up. A cold chill went through me. The mate to it was inside a small zipper compartment inside my purse."

For the rest of the trip, Casper kept a low profile. He did, however, follow the couple back home and, at that point, might have contributed to an additional haunting.

The presence of one ghost in an area can attract others, and Casper's long tenure seemed to have accomplished just that.

"A couple of years ago it wasn't just a simple little prank, so perhaps Casper had some rowdy friends. One night Jack saw two girls in long gowns, one at each corner of the foot of the bed. A third girl, dressed like an Indian princess, walked up to the head of the bed with a finger pointed at Jack then jabbed his forehead, leaving a small dark mark for a week. He jumped up and chased her into the bedroom's walk-in closet where she disappeared," Sarah recalled. "I woke up finding Jack in the closet looking behind the door and saying, 'She went in here.'"

Sarah also described a night when Jack woke up and "saw a tall man standing in the bedroom doorway. The man had his back to him. Jack reached out but [the image] disappeared."

Aside from those isolated nighttime visits by other spectres, Casper seems to be alone in his dimension, parallel to that of the couple he haunts.

For now, this is a ghost story without an ending. At least the ending hadn't been reached at the time of this writing, for Sarah, Jack and Casper continue to cohabit in an atmosphere of reciprocal, and respectful, acceptance.

Mysterious Manifestation

Tales of vanishing hitchhikers are staples of ghost lore. Anyone who's familiar with my book *Ghost Stories of the Rocky Mountains* will know that there are many reports of these mysterious manifestations. Despite the prevalence of these provocative entities, vanishing hitchhikers seemed to be under-represented in Alberta, the Highwood Hitchhiker being the only home-based example of the genre that I had come across.

When my publisher indicated that it was time to write this third book of Alberta ghost stories, I cast as wide an inquiry net as I could around the province. My efforts have been richly rewarded with all sorts of intriguing tales from every visible and invisible corner of Alberta. One of them was the following intriguing variation of the "vanishing hitchhiker" genre.

Roxie Wegenast wrote that she lives in the "rural county of Flagstaff, two hours southeast of Edmonton," more precisely on a "farm on Highway 36, approximately 12 miles [19 kilometres] south of Killam and northeast of Galahad."

After having first described the location, Roxie began to write about the event itself. "One evening, in the mid-1980s, I was returning home from a library board meeting in Galahad, driving north on Highway 36 toward our farm. I drove past a neighbour's farm that is just south of a coulee. As the highway continued down into the coulee, I had the inclination to turn my head to look at the passenger's seat. There was a young man sitting in my car!"

At this point in her message, Roxie certainly had my attention, just as, apparently, the intruder had hers! "I realized he wasn't flesh and blood, but, needless to say, I was scared. He appeared in shades of black, grey and white, as if a black-and-white movie was being projected into my car. His style of dress was early 1970s. He was wearing a black turtleneck, a mid-length coat, black leather boots, black pants and had straight, very blonde, chin-length hair parted down the middle."

The details of her description made me realize that the vision had really made an impression on the startled woman. All her senses must have been jolted into hypersensitivity because she had captured and retained so many particulars about the man.

"I could tell he was very pale even though he did not appear in colour. He had a very straight nose and was turned slightly towards me. He had a pleasant demeanour. All of these details I discerned in seconds. I turned back to the road, gripping the steering wheel very hard and repeating to myself, 'I did not see that. I did not see that.'"

Roxie's self-cautions were apparently effective against the seeming unreality that was, at that moment, her reality. "I turned to look again at the passenger's seat and he smiled and gave me a little wave of his hand. I looked back at the road and back again towards him—but, he was gone."

"There was nothing scary or threatening about the young man other than seeing him. I have told this story to friends and one woman believes she knows of people who had a similar encounter, also along Highway 36," my correspondent added.

She has looked into some local history and discovered that "there have been no accidents that we know of along that particular stretch of road."

For this reason, she wonders "if he could possibly [have been] making his way along the road to a destination."

What I found especially interesting about Roxie's experience was that she added, "up until that evening, if someone had told me this story, I would have dismissed them. My husband had always read ghost stories, but I had not really been interested. I was one of those individuals who thought there was a scientific explanation for everything. Since this encounter, I have heard stories from people I know well." These stories, Roxie acknowledged, "leave me with no doubt that ghosts are there if we care to see them."

I guess there's nothing like an actual encounter to turn a skeptic into a believer and, in this case, to put Alberta more squarely on the map for vanishing hitchhiker stories!

Harassed from Beyond

Nothing in Catherine's background prepared her for what she was forced to face in a northwest Calgary townhouse.

"I grew up on Cape Breton Island where ghosts and precognition were just taken for granted. It was very comforting," Catherine began to explain. "I've always known that there were places I felt welcomed in and places that I felt were best avoided. It was just a gut feeling and I always lived by that. At first I was so welcomed [at the Calgary townhouse]. I felt drawn there."

Catherine's feelings of contentment were about to change dramatically and abruptly. "Within a week of moving in I went from being happy to be there and feeling good about it to wanting to run in terror pulling my hair out. I felt completely terrorized."

From Catherine's description of the torment she endured, it seemed that she was a victim of ghostly harassment. "I was constantly being touched by things that I'm sure were children, things that were men. I got the distinct feeling from different touches that the place was full of people who shouldn't have been there. I was rubbing shoulders with people in hallways in our house."

Although Catherine felt that these beings touching her "were solid," she only ever saw one image, a woman. "She was real but she wasn't. Looking at her was looking at the face of death. She had her arms crossed. She was staring with little slits of eyes, the tiniest I've ever seen. She was waiting for someone. I don't think she was waiting for my babies but my son always had problems with that bedroom.

He would stand in the doorway, staring at the window, yelling 'Who are you people? Why are you here?'" Despite his strong reaction, the boy didn't seem to feel threatened by the presences.

As with most haunted houses, "there were times when my washing machine wouldn't start, when my dishwasher didn't work. My VCR actually broke."

Those instances were mere annoyances, however, compared to what was ahead.

"This might be the strangest. We were turning off the phone's ringer at night because it was a new number and we were getting a lot of wrong numbers. I didn't want that to waken my children. I was lying in bed on my right side. I heard a male speak into my left ear. The voice was from outside my head. It was not a thought. It told me that I should go and look at the phone. It was three o'clock in the morning. I lay there thinking about it for a long, long time. Finally, I had to get up and prove to myself that I must have been imagining things or hallucinating."

Unfortunately for Catherine's peace of mind, "the ring light was flashing on the phone. It was still ringing. The call display feature was showing 'unknown name, unknown number.' I couldn't bring myself to answer it. I didn't know what there'd be on the other end of the line."

Catherine's reaction was certainly understandable, especially after a disembodied voice had alerted her to the phone call in the first place.

If the spirits intended to chase Catherine out of her new home, they were successful. "I was so sick of it. It got to the point where I would see people and things and would get touched constantly. I had no idea where to turn. We left because I was not sleeping. I wasn't eating. How do you tell people you're moving because you're being sexually harassed by a ghost? We moved 44 days into a six-month lease and probably left two-thirds of our possessions behind. We've moved twice since then. The first time I felt like maybe I hadn't gotten rid of the emotional aura of that experience."

I wondered if the second move brought peace to her life, and Catherine answered, "I think our 'little friend' is back with us. The other night I had a bottle of shampoo dropped on my head in the bath. There's no way it could have just fallen because it would have had to have fallen up across the bathroom and then down again. I keep trying to brush this off, but I hear my cupboards opening and closing at night and my dishes rattle."

Not wanting to move yet again, Catherine began to seek advice from people she trusted. "Someone said to tell the spirit that I'm not concerned about sharing my home but just don't scare me. I tried that in the first house and it only got scarier. What's getting even stranger in this place is I have two friends who live in the same complex. One lives behind me, one lives in front of me. If you draw a line from the one behind me to the one in front of me, the line crosses right through my house and they're all having this problem when I'm around in some way. If I'm on the telephone with one of them, they'll be having manifestations in their home."

Catherine took a photograph of one of her new neighbours-cum-friends. When it was developed, she discovered "there was a someone in that picture who shouldn't have been there."

Catherine has casually investigated the background of that townhouse she fled. Both recent and distant histories proved to be interesting.

"I understand that the area has quite the checkered past. I've heard stories [about illegal activities going on there] so I can feel why there'd be residual energy. But, I don't know why it would be connected somehow to me. I had a neighbour who'd lived in the complex for nine and a half years. I asked her how many tenants had lived in our suite. She said the longest tenancy was about a year and the shortest was a few days. I haven't had the guts to go there to ask whoever's there now how they're liking it, I can't even face that place."

This poor beleaguered young woman has wisely decided that her energies would be better spent trying to rid herself completely of the negative spirits she picked up in the townhouse that cruelly conned her with their initial welcome.

Well-photographed Phantom

Calgarian W. Ritchie Benedict has developed his life-long interest in the supernatural into virtually an art form. He researches, writes and lectures on a wide range of paranormal topics, including ghosts. When *Fate Magazine* commissioned an article from Benedict about some of the haunted places around Calgary, they specified that they wanted him to take new photographs rather than use any he may have had on hand. In order to comply with this request, Benedict made arrangements to visit Prince House at Heritage Park in March 2000.

A figure seems to be standing at the 2nd floor window on the left, although no one was in the building at the time.

He didn't know it then, but the timing of his photo opportunity couldn't have been better, for he managed to capture the ghost of the Prince House on film. He took two pictures, roughly 15 seconds apart. In one, a ghostly image of the woman who haunts the house can be seen at a second floor window. In the other, she is gone.

The issue of *Fate Magazine* right after the one that ran Benedict's photos and article included a letter from Daniel Temme, who had been visiting Calgary from his home in Gerald, Missouri. A copy of an enlarged area of a photograph Temme had taken of the Prince House was also included. Sure enough, the image was there. This definitely surprised Temme, but anyone familiar with that particular ghost would know that her image has been captured in pictures on several occasions. In fact, one of the stories in my previous book, *More Ghost Stories of Alberta*, describes the success of another visitor to Prince House in capturing this phenomenon on film.

This photo, taken 15 seconds after the one on the previous page, shows that whatever figure was at the window before disappeared quickly.

Where's Wallace?

Tracy Roberts wrote to me from her home in High Prairie, Alberta, which is between and a little north of Slave Lake and Grande Prairie. She explained that her family had been directly connected with a ghost story for many years.

"It has always been retained through everyone's memories," Tracy began. "Since a lot of family it began with are no longer with us to retell the story, I felt it was due time to try to piece together what was left of this ghostly tale that we still live with to this day."

Tracy's sense of obligation to preserve oral history has meant that her family's ghost story can be recorded here as part of Alberta's ghost lore.

"It all began back in 1929 or 1930, west of High Prairie, in an area known as the Little Smoky Settlement. My ancestors began this settlement; I live here now with my husband and son along with my parents and my brother's family."

Tracy continued, "It was winter time, the snow was very deep. An old man came driving his team of horses into the settlement. My grandpa remembers that day, [for] the horses were literally leaping up with each stride to make it through the deep snow. They were pulling an old wagon with a mysterious-looking driver."

Part of the mystery surrounding the driver was simply that in such a small community, "everybody knows everybody but nobody recognized this man," Tracy explained. The stranger was a quiet man whose other difference was that he was blind. This would be an additional obstacle to his homesteading, but the stranger had come to the area to look for some land on which he could settle.

The man, whose name was Wallace, may have seemed odd to his new neighbours but he was apparently independent and resourceful, for not long after his arrival in the community, he found himself a place to live. Even after he was settled in, though, the newcomer kept to himself more than the established members of the community did and that only increased people's curiosity about him.

"There aren't many stories about Wallace's history. In fact we aren't even sure if 'Wallace' was his first name or last. He really was a mystery. He never even told anyone where he was from or why he came here. Some thought he may have come from England. The truth is, now, we'll never know," Tracy acknowledged. She added that she did "recall hearing a story that he used to have a little horse named Brownie that lived with him in his little shack of a house and, even though he was blind, he was always seen carrying a coal oil lantern with him."

"Embarrassingly enough," she continued, "I must confess that my grandfather and great-uncles began to tease him and play tricks on him. They took advantage of the fact that he couldn't see and did things like switching the sugar in his bowl for salt. I remember hearing the story of when Wallace was going to check his cattle. Because he was blind, he put bells on each of the animal's necks so he could find them when he rode out to the pasture in his wagon. One time the brothers got together and tied a cow bell to the underside of Wallace's wagon. That poor old man kept circling in the pasture calling to his cows, confused by the sound of the ring each time he'd move."

Wallace's departure from the area was as mysterious as his arrival. "It was as if, [one] night, Wallace just disappeared into thin air. There was no word to anyone that he had planned to leave the Little Smoky. It was shortly after that the ghost stories and sightings began. The stories are numerous through each generation of my family. They all claim to have seen the ghost of Wallace, lantern in hand, walking the fields of the Little Smoky again. Except they knew he was gone, so this time it was his ghost."

The apparition did seem to confirm one mystery surrounding Wallace. The ghost's very existence provided some confirmation that the man had died. Oddly, Wallace's ghost has never appeared to anyone other than those who teased him in life—or those, like Tracy, who were descended from those pranksters.

"My uncle recalls a story that gives him goosebumps to this day. It was back when he was a young man. The neighbours asked my uncle if he would ride out and tell other neighbours to come over for a community gathering that night."

Tracy's uncle was returning from this errand "when suddenly the horses stopped dead in their tracks. There on the road was a ghostly figure of an old man waving his arms."

The young man was never able to explain exactly what happened next. "It was almost as if he lost time [then] he suddenly remembered driving back into the yard of the house he had left just minutes before."

That experience may at least have prepared Tracy's uncle somewhat for what was to come. Every night, he and his father would go out to the barn and, after milking the cows, hang specific pieces of equipment on appropriately marked hooks. Often by the following morning, those things had been moved. Wallace's ghost was commonly credited with the annoying prank. "My grandpa used to say it was Wallace getting back at him for all the tricks he'd played" at the blind man's expense.

Tracy wrote that her father remembered one night when he was a young man and still living with his parents: "He was out driving the old tractor in the field late one warm evening. Suddenly, in the field ahead of him there was a light. It seemed to sway each time it came closer to him. He stopped and shut the tractor off, thinking that someone from the house was coming to talk to him. He called out to the light, but nobody answered. It just kept coming closer and closer without a sound. It was then that fear got the best of him and he bolted for the house. He threw open the door to find all the family sitting comfortably in the house. They looked at my father's face and said, 'It looks like you just saw a ghost!'"

Tracy remembers being told that her father replied, "I think I did!" He knew then that he'd seen Wallace's ghost.

More sightings of the mysterious apparition were yet to come. "Years later another uncle of mine was headed down the old Smoky road in his vehicle. A ghostly figure of an old man appeared out of nowhere. Frantically, the figure waved his hands. My uncle slammed on his brakes and the ghost disappeared right before his very eyes."

Wallace's paybacks did not stop with the generation of Tracy's family that knew him. "My brother and cousin were camping in the woods and they were visited by someone or something. The two boys were in their tent, just about to sleep, when suddenly a bright light appeared in the distance. Slowly, silently, it came closer and closer to the tent until the flickering light surrounded the tent, circling it, as if in search of a way inside. All of a sudden, the light just went out. After their fear had passed somewhat, the boys went out to investigate. There wasn't one sign at all of anyone being there," Tracy related and added that, to this day, those campers are convinced that they were visited by the lamp-carrying phantom.

As a teenager, Tracy, too, had an encounter with Wallace. "One time I had a bunch of friends out from school for a Ouija board party. We all climbed into my brother's truck and drove to an old abandoned yard in the Smoky. We climbed up into the rickety hayloft of an old barn and began trying to contact a spirit. Two of my friends, who had no knowledge of Wallace, were working the board when the pointer started to move. We asked what the spirit's name was. Slowly it began to spell W-A-L-L-A-C-E."

Of course, Tracy knew exactly whom they had contacted. After explaining the spirit's history and its connection with her family, the rudimentary séance continued. "Ask him if he'll show himself to us or give us a sign that he's here," the young woman recalled suggesting. She then explained the dramatic scene:

> To this day I regret getting them to ask that question. The pointer slowly made its way across the board and pointed to "YES" and then came to a stop. Quietly, we waited for our sign, not really sure what to expect. Suddenly we could hear a sound coming from the distance. We all flung our heads out of the hayloft opening. The moon was bright, but we couldn't see anything that might have been

making that sound. When [the phantom sound] was right underneath us it became crystal clear what we were hearing. It was the distinct sound of horse hooves galloping by, followed by the faint sound of squeaky wagon wheels. The sounds were there but there was nothing with them to see. It didn't take us long to stumble out of the hayloft and jump in the back of the truck. As we sped away we looked back through the trees. A glowing light was moving around the barn.

"The lantern! It's his lantern!" Tracy yelled. Her brother, who was driving, stopped the truck immediately and the youngsters all stared in terror at light coming from an empty building that had been abandoned years ago and had no power running in to it. By then the kids' "party" was effectively over.

Today Tracy has an interesting theory regarding the continuing presence of Wallace's ghost. She believes the man probably headed out in his horse-drawn wagon when he came to one of the many patches of muskeg on the road which was at that time a "crude undeveloped trail with a lot of muskeg or quicksand." Tracy explained, "I remember hearing stories of cattle lost in those sinkholes. About a mile down the road from where Wallace lived, there was a huge sinkhole. Farmers would dump loads and loads of gravel down there and the hole would just swallow it up. I believe that Wallace, heading out with his team of horses and wagon one night, got thrown into the mentioned sinkhole. His body slowly got buried over time as [locals] continued to dump stuff down into the hole.

Maybe that is why there was the sighting of an old man on the road waving his arms, looking for help."

Tracy is convinced that the ghost will be a part of the local culture for years to come: "As long as we continue to cross over his unsettled grave with our vehicles every day, I believe his spirit cannot rest."

Shared Sight

In the mid-1990s, Lisa and Gary, along with their two children, Sara, then six, and Byron, who was only one at the time, lived in the town of Sherwood Park, just east of Edmonton. The location was convenient for the family as Gary worked at the nearby Cooking Lake airport. Lisa was a stay-at-home mom. They were living a happy, almost idyllic existence when a coincidence occurred that shook these parents to the depths of their beings.

Little Sara was not a child prone to nightmares, Lisa explained, perhaps partly because she was "never allowed to watch anything frightening on television and we monitored everything she did."

The night the paranormal incident took place began as "a normal night," Lisa recalled. "Sara went to bed but I was awakened to bloodcurdling screams from her in the wee hours. She was sobbing and screaming that there was a man lying in blood by our bathroom door. There was a gun, she said, and lots of blood. I was horrified and took her to the bathroom, gave her a drink and reassured her there was nothing there. It took about 15 minutes to stop her from shaking.

"Gary was a heavy sleeper and that night slept through everything. The next morning Gary went to work. When he came home he gave me some horrible news. Gary's boss's brother-in-law [who lived in British Columbia] had shot himself that same night in front of his six-year-old daughter."

As Lisa listened to her husband, she realized "the details all matched what Sara had told me that night. I feel Sara somehow saw through the eyes of this other young girl."

We will probably never know how the dreadful event, witnessed by a six-year-old girl in another province, transmitted itself to Sara. Fortunately the horrible vision was not a precursor for Lisa's daughter—her mother concluded her retelling with the assertion that "Sara is now almost 14 and nothing [else] out of the ordinary has happened [to her] since."

Megan's Manifestation

The first time I received a letter from a reader thanking me for the comfort that one of my ghost story books brought her, I was surprised. By now I've come to expect to receive at least one such letter with each new book. Inevitably, these people who write to me have felt relieved to read about others who'd had experiences similar to their own strange encounters. Some of these readers declared that, up until then, they had kept their paranormal encounters secret for fear of what people would think of them. Others actually went so far as to indicate that they had originally been concerned about their sanity—until they read that others had also been involved with inexplicable circumstances.

Linda McBride, of Calmar, contacted me with a different twist on that theme. It struck Linda that telling me of her experience with a ghost might enable her to get a comforting message to bereaved parents.

"Your book might be the perfect instrument," Linda began, "maybe the mom or dad of the little girl will read your book."

Setting the background, Linda explained, "It started in 1985, in the late summer or early fall. We had just moved into a new home in the Lee Ridge area of Millwoods [on Edmonton's south side]. One night I woke up and, the way our bedroom was arranged, I could see into the walk-in closet."

This, Linda explained, was her first sighting of the ghost that was to haunt her for years to come. "She was a young girl, probably about 12 or 13 years old. She had short brown hair. She was wearing a white T-shirt and those blue and white silky shorts" that were fashionable in the early 1980s.

Linda could not think of anyone she knew who had died at that age. She initially thought that the spirit might have been a "dear friend of someone who lived in the house before."

Seeing the ghostly image made Linda feel as though she may have somehow intruded on a visitation intended for someone else, so she manufactured an opportunity to ask the previous owners of the house if they might have had a young girl in their lives who had died.

"They looked at me as though I was nuts," the personable woman acknowledged before stating flatly, "They were wrong, though."

Linda was convinced of what she'd seen, that the vision of the girl was real. It was so real that, for no reason that she understood at the time, Linda began to call the spectral image "Megan." The child became a regular visitor. "I used to feel this little child's presence. She would reek of chocolate, a chocolate smell so strong that it was nauseating. It made me lightheaded. It was like this child had melted chocolate all over her hands and was trying to crawl up on me. When I would stop through my day and sit down for a cup of coffee she would always be trying to crawl up on my lap. This happened a lot and I felt bad because I could tell that this was a child, a little child who wanted to be comforted. It happened often."

Linda continued, "At the time I had three dogs at home. I used to feel a dog near me. I'd look down but there was no dog there. Also during this time my sister and I were taking classes to try to learn to meditate. One time after class, my sister suggested that I ask the instructor, a well-known psychic named Alex, if he could clue in on what was happening to me."

Linda reinforced, "Remember, Alex didn't know me [but] he said to me, 'You used to work in a doctor's office.'"

The man's words were a shock to the woman with the invisible visitor for she had, indeed, worked both in a dental office and an office of physicians. It was Alex's next statement, however, that shocked Linda to the core of her being. "The girl's name is Megan," he told her, echoing the name that she had intuitively used for the ghost. "She and her dog died in a very severe, horrible car accident. She came to you because she felt safe."

But why, Linda wondered, would such a little girl feel particularly drawn to her? Alex seemed to know: "When you were working in a doctor's office she used to sit on your lap."

There was no denying the truth of that statement, Linda conceded. "There were a couple of kids who did that because they were so scared. I remember one, she only came to us once but she was so terrified, this poor little thing, she asked if she could sit on my lap. Of course, I let her."

And the invisible dog that Linda was frequently aware of was, according to Alex's psychic reading of the haunting, Megan's dog. "She's laughing and telling you that's her dog," Alex explained before adding that the child's soul had a message for someone on this plane. She wanted it known that until "somebody had come for her she had waited with me and that she was fine."

Alex had given Linda a great deal to think about after that meditation class. Their conversation was winding down to a natural close when, in a puzzled tone of voice, the man asked, "Can you smell chocolate?"

Badly shaken by this impromptu psychic reading and the new burdens upon her that it implied, Linda pondered her next move. Because she felt she had a responsibility to relay the message that her phantom guest was extending, the sensitive woman thought of going through files in the medical office where she'd been employed. This might have been an effective way to find the entity's parents, but a flood in that office had destroyed some of the records. Besides, as Linda put it, "Even if I find her file, how do I phone and ask, 'Did you have a daughter who died?'"

Knowing herself and accepting her emotional limitations, Linda realized that she "didn't have the courage to do that so I let it go." Or, at least, she tried to let thoughts of the presence go.

Even though the childish vision no longer visits her, "quite frankly the thought of her has stayed with me through all these years. I still get goosebumps when I think about it. I still talk to her every now and again. I've felt bad because I should've followed this through. It's a lot of years later and I know they must have gone through a lot of torment. I think it was grandparents who came for her."

In the hopes that little Megan's parents might recognize their daughter through Linda's descriptions and be comforted by the fact that she's been escorted to a safe place beyond, the woman shared her experiences with me for this book.

Employed Entity

Once the most sought-after office address in downtown Edmonton, the stately architectural edifice on 100th Street now stands all but deserted. In its prime, however, the nine-storey building dominated the city's downtown landscape and was as impressive on the inside as on the outside. In 1912, when the building was being constructed, no expense was spared. Extravagances such as Italian marble and the finest in hardwoods were used throughout. This was clearly a place where important matters were handled.

The last tenants in the old place were non-profit organizations that appreciated the rock-bottom rental rates. Before they vacated their digs, a few employees spoke of ghostly encounters. From their stories, and those of a night watchman named Jim, it would seem that not all of the previous tenants have left.

Among the amenities that made the office tower so appealing to its first occupants were the elevators, which, in keeping with the times, were operated by attendants. Today we may think that operating an elevator all day long would've been boring, but in those days the job was looked upon as a position of some privilege. Elevator operators proudly wore almost military-like uniforms and were deemed by building owners and occupants to be indispensable. At least one such employee at this office building is thought to have remained on duty—even after death.

Jim, the security guard I spoke with, told me, "The elevator would go up and down by itself." Other former occupants said that you could not always be sure the elevator would stop at the floor that you wanted to go to. Any who found themselves going along for a spirited joyride could at least be confident that they were safe. An operator dedicated enough to stay on after death would, no doubt, protect the elevator's patrons.

A man related an incident that occurred at the ninth-floor suite where he worked. Co-workers told him that they were unable to open the office door one day. The door, which had always swung freely before, simply would not budge, no matter how hard either of them pushed on it. Seconds later the mail slot in the door "shot open." The pair felt a surge of air rush past them and seconds later the flap on the mail slot slammed closed. Immediately after that burst of seemingly inexplicable activity, the errant door opened as easily as it had every other time either one of them had entered the office.

Others who worked in the building during the early 1990s acknowledged that they often had the sensation that they were not alone when their usually reliable five senses indicated that they were.

A woman who witnessed an apparition but would not reveal her identity explained in some detail that, when she was in a hallway, she caught a glimpse of what she initially suspected was an intruder. Certainly, it was a person she'd never seen before in the building. She saw him clearly. He had a moustache and wore glasses. Then, as she stared with some concern at the image, it vanished. It simply disappeared before her eyes.

The experience may have startled the woman but it is unlikely that the ghost-sighting scared her, for Jim stressed that he found the entity was simply "playful."

Illusion in the Living Room

Daphne and I were discussing a topic not connected with my search for "new" Alberta ghost stories. Once our transaction had come to an end, though, she mentioned something that I found especially intriguing.

"For many years we lived in a house in Calgary which was built in 1911," the charming woman began before explaining that the home's original owner was an influential community leader. "My husband always felt that the walls were full of political intrigue. An elderly friend of ours told us that when she visited us she would often see a woman dressed in older clothes, sitting in the living room, pouring tea. I certainly didn't doubt it. All our friends were aware of the lady."

Daphne does wonder, however, where the spirit might have fled to after they sold their haunted home. "The house has since been completely gutted and redone. I wonder whether she is still there or whether she is possibly mourning the loss of her home."

We can only hope that the long-deceased lady has, by now, found a place at least as comfortable as what was probably her former home.

A Noisy Pair

In 1990, when it was new, this house in Calgary's northwest was definitely "on the edge of town." It was also most assuredly haunted.

"They would take things," my informant stated about the ghosts. "You'd search the whole house for your keys and then you'd find them in the middle of the kitchen floor."

And then there were the sounds of disembodied footfalls that could never quite be tracked down. "You'd hear footsteps in one room but when you ran in there the noises would be coming from another room. You got to the point that you were chasing this thing around."

But, of course, "it" would never be caught. Part of the reason for the intensity of spirit activity in that house was that there was, apparently, more than one entity residing there. The owners' teenage daughter recalled a time when she was in the bathroom and noticed that some small article had suddenly gone missing. In anger she shouted to the spirits, "If you're so real, why don't you just show yourself?"

As the youngster opened the bathroom door she stared in disbelief at the floor just beyond. There, standing together, were a pair of men's shoes and a pair of women's shoes. The girl only looked up a little farther—enough to see that there were feet in these shoes and legs attached above those—before she slammed the bathroom door closed and locked herself in until another member of her family came home. By that time, the spirits had disappeared again.

The family found ways to work around the ghosts. If the spirits were restless, someone's piano playing usually settled them down. When the piano music was accompanied by the steady beat of a metronome, the ethereal tenants made their presences known again. If the musician either slowed or quickened his pace, the metronome did the same.

With the rapid expansion that the city of Calgary's gone through, it's a sure bet that this house could no longer be described as being "on the edge of town." Whether or not it is still as haunted is something only the current occupants know for sure.

The Mystery of Retrocognition

Many of us have heard of, and even experienced, the phenomenon of precognition—of seeing or sensing something that is about to happen. There are times, for instance, when you "know" your friend is about to call—and then, just a few minutes later, that call comes through. Or, you dream vividly about an event that then comes to pass a few days later. These are examples of precognition.

Retrocognition is virtually the opposite. It is a phenomenon that allows us a glimpse into the past. Dramatic examples of retrocognition have been documented for years from places all around the globe. Some students of the paranormal suggest that every ghost sighting is in fact a retrocognitive experience. Others are sure that in our everyday lives we all encounter retrocognition, but because it is often fleeting it is over too quickly for us to recognize the sensation for what it is. As a result, we tend to discount and forget the event.

A few retrocognitive occurrences are well documented and have been witnessed by numerous people over the years. Just to the south of Alberta, portions of the Battle at Little Bighorn have replayed themselves spontaneously in front of modern-day visitors to the site of Custer's Last Stand. In the Canadian town of Niagara-on-the-Lake, three injured soldiers slowly make their way back to camp along a route called Lundy's Lane. There's no way that anyone can help these men, for they are returning from a battle that was part of the War of 1812.

There are also recorded instances of retrocognition here in Alberta. One of the most dramatic firsthand accounts I've ever been told comes from an elderly widow who now lives in Gibbons, Alberta. She wrote to me of a time when she and her husband were newlyweds camping in the Mercoal area of Alberta's Coal Branch.

"One night when the moon rose we walked into [an] open area. Suddenly [there appeared, straight ahead]— a train headlight!"

Apparently their spirit of adventure was greater than their fear, for, showing admirable courage, the wife suggested, "'Let's join hands and stand still.' It came at us—and ran right through us. We looked back and saw its tail end."

Fascinated by their strange experience, the couple spoke of it often, during the rest of their camping trip as well as when they returned home. As neither of them was able to shake the sense that something extraordinary had happened to them that day, they decided to investigate. Their research efforts were rewarded when they discovered that a railway line had once run through the spot where they'd been standing. The light they saw, the light that passed through them, had not actually shone for many, many years. It was a phantom light. They had experienced retrocognition.

A more recent example of this phenomenon came to my attention from a correspondent in Ontario who had heard about two young women in an unidentified small town in Alberta. They were neighbours who had become friends and often drove to and from work together. On one of those trips the pair had an experience they'll never forget.

Kathy, who was relating the anecdote, noted that as the route was so familiar to them, neither was paying much attention to the scenery as they drove along. Kathy was driving, her thoughts wandering, when her companion tapped her on her shoulder.

"Have you ever seen this place?" the passenger asked.

Kathy stopped the car. She looked all around her and could not believe her eyes. It was as though they'd left the modern-day world. Instead of concrete sidewalks, there were wooden boardwalks, the streets were unpaved and people were dressed in what Kathy and her friend considered "period" clothing. The buildings were of an era 100 years prior—complete with proud and freshly painted false fronts.

An uncomfortable atmosphere began to build within Kathy and her friend as they realized they were glimpsing history. Seconds later, they turned the car around and headed away from the retrocognitive scene. As they drove, they kept checking in the car's mirrors to see what sort of image was behind them. Slowly the out-of-sync scene "seemed to shimmer and fade, and disappear" Kathy related. Then, as they continued to drive, the two realized that their "present town began to take its place."

It's pretty clear that Kathy and her friend, like other people in other places, had experienced retrocognition.

Spirit Snippets

In August 2000, I was delighted to once again be a guest on CBC AM's early afternoon phone-in show. People from all over the province called in to share unexplainable, possibly supernatural, experiences they'd had over the years. Unfortunately, there were still callers waiting to get through on the phone lines when we ran out of the time available to that program. The calls we were able to take, however, made up a fascinating assortment of supernatural incidents from all over the province.

Alva from Edson was the first caller on the line. She related an encounter that she was sure she understood, that comforted rather than frightened her, and yet she knew it was a ghost story.

"In 1953, when my husband and I were first married, we lived by a man and his wife and their four children. They were dear friends of ours," Alva began.

Sadly, the neighbour woman died prematurely. The grieving husband took his children and moved away, selling the former family home to Alva and her husband before he left town.

"We moved in and one night when I was sleeping I felt a presence. I felt really relaxed and happy about it. I was sure it was her [Alva's friend who had just died] who had come back to say, 'That's fine, I'm glad you're in my house.' She stroked my hair reassuringly, so gently. I sensed her presence. I sensed that it was she who was there."

That visitation was a "one-time occurrence," Alva explained, but she also acknowledged, "I know my father's spirit comes to me in this house. When I'm sitting alone in the evening I feel a cool breeze and smell his tobacco smoke. He comes to see me occasionally."

Jill now lives in Edmonton but remembered a summer when she lived in Calgary while working at an institution for autistic children. The place was widely accepted as being haunted by a former resident.

"I never saw the ghost but a number of people who work there *have* seen the image," Jill began. "A child died there. Almost all of the staff who work there have seen the ghost and I'm inclined to believe what they say. These people are credible."

The image apparently manifests as a "white glowing form walking up and down the hallway. They said it had some of the same mannerisms as an autistic child."

Perhaps the staff should be reassured by the presence. The little one so enjoyed his stay at the residence in life that he returned to it after death.

Lesley, from Edmonton, called to tell us that she and others who had worked in Edson at the museum known as the Red Brick School House suspected that the school, constructed in 1913, was haunted. "Often on weekends we'd have to work by ourselves and you could hear people walking around upstairs in the classroom even though there was no one in the school. One Saturday I heard a voice where I was standing at the door of the gift shop. It said, 'Hi.' It sounded like a little girl who had been dared to or something because it was a high-pitched, squeaky little 'Hi.' I went looking around trying to see if there was anyone around but there was no one in the place at all."

Other workers apparently "heard people walking and there had been problems with all the light bulbs burning out at the same time."

While she acknowledged that working in an apparently haunted building could be unnerving, Lesley did adapt to it. "My Dad would tell me, 'Say hi to the kids for me when you get there.' That's what it seemed like, a bunch of kids, at least a few." Or perhaps, more correctly, the ghosts of a bunch of kids.

Barb called in to tell us about a ghost named Oscar who lived in the Crowsnest Pass—in an old church in the well-haunted town of Hillcrest, to be specific. "The church is closed down now," she told us. People wonder where Oscar might have gone, for he used to make his presence known quite frequently by manifesting as an apparition and by moving stuff in church. As Barb said, "Once he even started up a worker's saw."

Perhaps Oscar has joined the many other spirits from that area of coal mining disasters.

On Halloween 2000, I had a great time with Margie Taylor, host of CBC AM's early afternoon show, taking calls from listeners all over the province who believed that they'd had experiences with ghosts. The following story, from a Calgary woman who identified herself as Jessica, was one of the intriguing anecdotes we heard that day.

Jessica began simply by stating, "I had the spirit of a young child follow me around for about a year and a half."

It was clear from the tone in her voice and her description of the events that Jessica wasn't frightened by the presence of her ghostly companion. Quite the contrary—it seemed she rather enjoyed the little fellow. With a minimum of prompting from either Margie or me, the caller continued, "This was only about four years ago. It wouldn't haunt anyone else, just me. It wasn't demonic or evil or bad, just mischievous. He just wanted someone to play with."

Of course, the obvious question to pose to Jessica at that point in the conversation was "How did you know you had a ghost with you?" In answering, the woman acknowledged that it had taken her "a little while to figure this out," but then she went on to explain that "every once in a while in that state between wake and sleep, all of a sudden I'd be jolted out of falling gently asleep." After a few instances like that, combined with "times when I put something down and knew that I had put it in a certain place [but] when I went back to get it, it wasn't there anymore," Jessica reported that she had begun to suspect something supernatural was at work.

Sometime later, the haunted woman decided it would be fun to visit a psychic fair that was in town for the weekend. "I wasn't even thinking about [the ghost] at the time. I had my cards read and the reader told me, 'You have a spirit following you. Are you noticing that things are missing?'"

Jessica assured the card reader that such was definitely the case. It was then that she learned more about her constant companion. "I found out it was a little boy around four or five years old who had passed away but didn't know what to do. He was just playing games."

Once Jessica had verification of her suspicions, she decided to help the youngster's soul move on to a more appropriate plane of existence. She explained to us that she told the spirit, "Okay, your time's up here. You need to go and pass through the light." The boy's soul apparently heeded Jessica's urgings. Although the child's ghost ceased to be a presence in her life, her months with him will always live on in her memory.

Jessica related a second incident in her life that illustrated how difficult it is for us humans to objectively describe a paranormal encounter.

"My grandfather passed away ... in a hospice. We knew that he was dying. The day before he died was Christmas day. I was driving home to get Christmas presents and he— well, his spirit—was in the car with me. I heard him saying,

'Keep going, keep doing what you want to do today because you need that. Make sure the whole family's there.' Then he put his hand on my hand [which was] on the parking brake. When I turned to look, he was gone."

Fascinated by the report of this interchange between the living and the dying, I asked Jessica if she had heard the man's voice externally or merely inside her head. She replied, "It's hard to describe. It was probably in my mind but I heard it outside."

Although at the beginning of her call, Jessica had indicated that she had encountered several spectral beings over the course of her life, the time constraints of radio broadcasts meant that we were unable to hear about her other experiences. Her situations, however, certainly lent credence to the theory that some people are very much more likely than others to perceive psychic phenomena.

Cheryl, calling from Ponoka, wanted to relate the story of her sister's haunted house "out in the country."

"It started very simply with things going missing." Cheryl recalled that her sister had told her things like keys would be put down in one place but not found there when they were needed again.

Then the haunting began to escalate. An unseen and unheard force would "move all the bottles and containers around" the edge of the bathtub, and "lights would go on and off."

As is often the case under these circumstances, family members began blaming one another for carelessness.

When Cheryl's sister would find a light on that should have been turned off she would blame her daughter, telling her "Don't leave the light on." Unfortunately, her scolding never did any good—because the child's mother was addressing the wrong source. The lights continued to turn on and off even though no one had been near any switches.

The most dramatic episode almost mimicked the events of the movie *Toy Story* when her child's battery-operated toys "began coming on in the middle of the night." Hearing Cheryl describe a stuffed replica of Big Bird seemingly coming to life was, indeed, chilling.

Supporting the theory that some people are more likely than others to have a ghostly encounter, Cheryl also revealed that many suspected her cousin's home in Calgary had also been haunted. "Her washing machine would start up when no one had turned it on."

Although that is a pretty standard ghostly activity, this particular ghost was unique in that it roamed between two houses and was active in both. Cheryl's cousin "would be walking up her steps and hear the stereo come on. It would get louder and louder. Bathtub (faucets) would turn on by themselves." Cheryl described the height of the haunting in her cousin's house:

> It kind of all came to a head one night when my 13-year-old niece got up in the morning and said, "Mom were you in my room last night? I woke up and saw someone looking down at me, was it you?" That really freaked her mother out that time but then it settled down for a while. It got started again when

the baby arrived on the scene. There was new energy in the home then. Now there's another baby in the home again and things are kind of starting up again. The chair in that room is rocking. The first child, who's now three years old, absolutely refused to sleep in that bedroom and, of course, as is typical, that room is much colder than any other room.

Frustratingly, at that point in the call, the demands of radio scheduling meant that I was not able to learn whether these hauntings in Cheryl's family were ongoing or whether they had subsided.

A southside community of Edmonton, now referred to as "*Old* Strathcona," was not even a part of the city until 1912, seven years after Alberta became a province. Today, some of the original residences, from the days when Strathcona was a separate town, still stand and are coveted pieces of real estate.

A caller named Judy was fortunate enough to have been living in one of those stately old homes for nearly a quarter century. The story she wished to relate dated back to her family's earliest days in the house when they had just begun the process of restoring the place to its original dignity. She didn't realize, for the first few months, that she'd bought a haunted house.

"My youngest daughter was born in 1977. The room that she was to use had been the room of a daughter of the original family. This young woman, back in the early 1900s, had a child when she wasn't married. Of course, that was not considered to be proper," Judy began. "After my [youngest] daughter was born, my second daughter, whose room was across the hall, used to talk about this nice lady who used to come and tuck them in at night."

When the little girls were telling their mother about these events, they always added emphatically, "It wasn't you and it wasn't the babysitter. It was this nice lady."

The mystery lady's visits kept up long enough that, to this day, Judy's daughters have memories of her and her comforting nocturnal calls.

Judy had evidently put some effort into learning the history of her "new" house.

"Before she passed away, I had met the woman whose room it had been in the early 1900s. I really do believe it was she who was coming to care for my two youngest children at night in this big old house. She was a gentle presence and very positive. No one ever felt threatened but you'd often see something out of the corner of your eye when the house was quiet. I'm sure it was she who came to tuck the girls in."

In the nicest possible way, Judy's daughters grew up with a bit of "living" history.

When Michael called CBC's "Midday Express" program in August 2000, he was an adult living in Hinton. He vividly recalled, though, an incident that took place in the late 1960s when he was a teenager growing up in the town of Drumheller.

As part of a traditional rite of passage, Michael and his friends spent many summer nights out camping. They chose different campsites over the years, but there was one that none of them would ever forget.

"We were just a young bunch of guys out camping," Michael explained. "But we kept smelling perfume all night. We thought it was one of the guys. Poor Harvey, we bugged him then and for weeks after [saying] that he was wearing perfume."

Their teasing came to a stop, however, after they had the opportunity to speak with a local historian "by the name of Jessie Jackson." She knew the rather sordid history of the land the boys had camped on. Long ago, she explained, a house of ill repute was located there.

Michael continued, "She told me that the place had been haunted and that [the ghost] was one of the girls who'd apparently died down there. The building's not standing anymore, but it was a particularly neat place to go camping."

Perhaps that was so—for everyone but poor Harvey!

An employee at a used book store in the Old Strathcona area of Edmonton had a most interesting story to tell me. He claimed that the owner of the store was sure the place was haunted. His reasoning for this belief was that often when he opened the store in the mornings, a copy of my book *Ghost Stories of Alberta*, which had been in its proper place on a shelf the night before, would be lying on the floor by the door!

Collect the whole series!

North America's colourful history is full of spine-tingling ghost tales that will have you checking under the bed, behind closet doors and in the basement. Haunting tales involve many well-known theatres, buildings and landmarks, many of which are still being used. Stories range from the return of long-dead relatives, to phantom footsteps in unused attics, to whispers of disembodied voices from behind the walls.

Canadian Ghost Stories	1-55105-302-0
Ghost Stories and Mysterious Creatures of British Columbia	1-55105-172-9
Ghost Stories of California	1-55105-237-7
Ghost Stories of Christmas	1-55105-334-9
Ghost Stories of Hollywood	1-55105-241-5
Ghost Stories of Illinois	1-55105-239-3
Ghost Stories of Manitoba	1-55105-180-X
Ghost Stories of Texas	1-55105-330-6
Ghost Stories of the Maritimes	1-55105-329-2
Ghost Stories of the Old West	1-55105-332-2
Ghost Stories of the Rocky Mountains	1-55105-165-6
Ghost Stories of Washington	1-55105-260-1
More Ghost Stories of Alberta	1-55105-083-8
More Ghost Stories of Saskatchewan	1-55105-276-8
Ontario Ghost Stories	1-55105-203-2

$14.95 each

Available at your local bookseller or from Lone Pine Publishing:
Phone: 1-800-661-9017 • Fax: 1-800-548-1169